BUILDING BUSINESS VALUE THROUGH TALENT

Tom McGuire and Linda Brenner draw on unique backgrounds spanning senior roles in operations, finance, and human resources to master the intersection of talent and market value. With *Building Business Value through Talent* they have created a common framework and language that finally optimizes the essential CEO and CHRO partnership in our knowledge economy.

> – **Jack Stahl**, Co-Founder of CNEXT; a Virtual Mentoring Platform for Senior Leaders, Corporate Board Member, Private Equity Advisor, former CEO of Revlon, and President of The Coca-Cola Company

The connection between HR and business valuation has been nebulous until now. This guide informs a CEO how enterprise value, intellectual capital, and talent are linked – and how to take practical, measurable actions to maximize results with this in mind. HR no longer needs to worry about "having a seat at the table" – this proves that their role in our knowledge economy requires them to host the party.

> – **Harold Osborn**, President and Chief Executive Officer, McIlhenny Company

It is easy to think of Finance as the steward of financial capital, and Operations as the steward of tangible assets. Tom and Linda's book shows HR how to be the steward of intellectual capital, which accounts for more than 80% of market valuation. Tom and Linda lay out clearly and conversationally, both the areas on which HR should focus to maximize this stewardship, as well as how the CEO should partner with HR to maximize the market cap of their company. With the ever-increasing influence of Talent on market valuation, *Building Business Value Through Talent* should be required reading for executives everywhere.

> – **Andrew Lobo**, CHRO C2 Educational Systems, former CHRO at Arhaus, Inc.

Finally, an approach that proves the value of talent investments and guides HR decision-making in a data-based, value-creating way. This framework recognizes the critical connection between finance and talent that has been missing for far too long. This guide acts as a roadmap for positioning HR as the key to growing business value.

– **Deborah McFarlane**, Chief People Officer at EmployBridge, former head of HR for HD Supply Facilities Maintenance.

Tom and Linda have developed what will become the standard operating model for CEO and CHRO partnerships. What I appreciate most is that they have combined their practitioner backgrounds, along with their deep expertise in finance and talent management, to develop a value-added framework and guide for prioritizing, operationalizing, and measuring the true value of HR investments. They approach the work with a real-world perspective and this approach is long overdue.

– **Stacey Valy Panayiotou**, EVP-HR for Graphic Packaging International, former senior talent management, HR, Diversity & Inclusion and Organization Effectiveness leader for The Coca-Cola Company and Coca-Cola Enterprises, Inc.

BUILDING BUSINESS VALUE THROUGH TALENT

The CEO and CHRO Partnership Guide

BY

THOMAS MCGUIRE
Talent Growth Advisors, USA

LINDA BRENNER
Talent Growth Advisors, USA

United Kingdom – North America – Japan
India – Malaysia – China

Emerald Publishing Limited
Howard House, Wagon Lane, Bingley BD16 1WA, UK

First edition 2021

Reprints and permissions service
Contact: permissions@emeraldinsight.com

British Library Cataloguing in Publication Data
A catalogue record for this book is available from the British Library

ISBN: 978-1-80043-116-4 (Print)
ISBN: 978-1-80043-115-7 (Online)
ISBN: 978-1-80043-117-1 (Epub)

ISOQAR certified
Management System,
awarded to Emerald
for adherence to
Environmental
standard
ISO 14001:2004.

Certificate Number 1985
ISO 14001

INVESTOR IN PEOPLE

CONTENTS

LIST OF FIGURES

LIST OF TABLES

LIST OF TABLES

ABOUT THE AUTHORS

Thomas McGuire is unique in the talent management world as a person who has been both a Chief Financial Officer and a Global Talent Acquisition Director at well-known consumer product, NYSE companies.

Tom has 40 years of business experience following his first job out of college as a Peace Corps Volunteer in Central America. He began his business career as an external auditor in Columbus, Ohio, and after becoming a C.P.A. in 1982, left Coopers & Lybrand to join The Coca-Cola Company.

Tom spent his first years at Coke traveling around the world as an international auditor, followed by Corporate Finance roles supporting Latin America, Europe, and Africa. He assumed the Finance leadership role in the company's German Division in 1990 following the fall of the Berlin Wall. After playing a key role expanding Coke's business into the former East Germany, Tom returned to Atlanta in 1993 to work as part of the marketing management team reporting to the Chief Marketing Officer, Sergio Zyman. In addition to managing marketing financial plans, Tom was responsible for rebranding the World of Coca-Cola and Company Stores, building the WOCC Las Vegas and expanding the licensed merchandise business of the company. As a Vice-President in Coke's Marketing Division, Tom played a key role negotiating worldwide advertising agreements that led the way in establishing the industry trend toward fee-based compensation with agencies. From 1997 to 1999 Tom led the Global Talent Acquisition function at Coca-Cola, sourcing general management and marketing talent for worldwide operations and all talent for North America. In 1999 he moved into a role in Latin America, leading the development of a market-level strategy and integration plan for Peru following Coke's acquisition of Inca Cola.

In 2000 Tom joined Zyman Marketing Group in Atlanta, a developer of web-based marketing tools, as Chief Operating Officer. Following Zyman Marketing Group he formed a consulting venture, Human Capital Formation, LLC. In this business Tom provided consulting services that guided the redesign of the human resources functions and processes at clients including Children's Healthcare of Atlanta and Emory Healthcare.

In 2003, Tom joined Revlon, Inc., in New York City, serving as Revlon's Chief Financial Officer and then as President, Revlon International. During his tenure at Revlon, Tom led multiple debt and equity financing transactions totaling more than $2 billion, built the company's investor relations function, and implemented procedures to comply with Sarbanes–Oxley and other SEC mandated reporting requirements.

Tom rejoined the Coca-Cola Company in October 2007 as Group Director, Global Talent Acquisition, and focused on supporting the company's growth by developing and executing strategies to acquire top professional talent and independent contractors in the company's markets around the world. He built a globally based internal search firm at Coke and designed and implemented systematic measurement of talent quality for external hiring.

Tom retired from Coca-Cola and has worked with Linda Brenner since 2013, cofounding Talent Growth Advisors with Linda in 2015.

He and his wife Chris have been married 38 years and have 3 children: Olivia, Sean, and Patrick. In his free time Tom enjoys road biking, playing guitar and other instruments, and writing and recording music.

tom@talentgrowthadvisors.com

Linda Brenner cofounded Talent Growth Advisors with the vision of helping business leaders improve talent results. The firms' clients include great brands such as Coca-Cola, Tabasco, Amazon, The Home Depot, Chick-fil-A, Raytheon, Microsoft, and Ogilvy.

Linda's innovative, results-oriented approach is coupled with a bias for action and a focus on measurable results. This same orientation is reflected throughout the TGA team of talent acquisition, talent management, and finance experts.

Prior to Talent Growth Advisors, Linda spent her professional career leading talent acquisition and talent management teams for Gap, Pepsi/Pizza Hut, and The Home Depot. Linda held a variety of roles at The Home Depot, including leader of enterprise-wide talent management practices including succession planning, talent review, and 360° feedback. Subsequently, she was then tapped to lead the company's talent acquisition centralization effort. In addition to centralizing TA for the first time in the company's history, under

Linda's leadership, The Home Depot also became the largest government contractor in the United States and forged first-of-their-kind partnerships with AARP, the Department of Defense, and the Department of Labor.

Prior to The Home Depot, Linda was with the Pizza Hut organization when it was still part of the Pepsi enterprise. There, she held a variety of roles, including HR generalist, national staffing manager, and the division's training and development group leader. At Gap, early in her career, she held operational roles in the Northeast division, including running the highest volume store there, until she moved to the company's San Francisco headquarters to lead a management development effort aimed at improving store performance.

Over the years, Linda has demonstrated a unique ability to break complex problems into manageable pieces and has led many teams to drive results in a timely, measurable, and results-oriented way. She works closely with business leaders and HR partners to create the business case, consensus, and tactical plan for change.

Linda holds a Master of Arts degree in Labor and Employment Relations and a Bachelor of Arts degree in Judaic Studies, both from University of Cincinnati. She and her family live in Atlanta.

linda@talentgrowthadvisors.com

The proper man understands equity, the small man profits.
Confucius (551–479 BC)

CHAPTER SUMMARIES

Important Instructions
At the Intersection of Talent and Market Value

This introductory chapter updates history, data, and formula for calculating the value of companies and the direct connection between Intellectual Capital, the largest component of market value, and specific critical talent within organizations. It is the foundation for tapping into the strategic opportunity presented to CEOs and CHROs.

Features at a Glance
Strategic Talent Function and Tools

This chapter describes in detail specific functions and tools of HR and how they directly impact value creation, whether or not the organization itself is fully cognitive of that impact in current state. Combined with the introductory chapter, the formula for creating value through talent, and the roles of CEO and CHRO in doing that, are revealed.

Installation
How to Start or Restart the Strategic HR Function

This chapter outlines how business value is created and its inescapable link to HR and, specifically, talent. We dive into methodologies for either building a customized HR function from scratch or transforming the existing function into an investment vehicle rather than an administrative cost.

Controls
The Most Important Facets of the HR Operating Model and How They Can Be Monitored

The ability to execute on HR initiatives is pointless without understanding what success looks like for the business and having the means to monitor progress and remediate shortcomings. The ubiquity of data in modern HR organizations can easily overwhelm and not effectively aid in making the highest priority decisions and course corrections. This chapter identifies the stages of execution and delivery in the HR Operating Model that are most essential to ensuring successful investment outcomes.

Changing the Filter
Refreshing the HR Operating Model Over Time

Even the ideal HR Operating Model today will not withstand the test of time for very long – the lens through which the model is viewed must be attuned with the business' evolving vision of itself. Since businesses are valued on future potential rather than past performance, this chapter spells out how to ensure your talent strategy is future focused and maximizes business value.

Care and Maintenance
Actions Taken Periodically to Keep the HR Operating Model in Working Order

Rather than going through a painful and inefficient cycle of off-and-on HR investment which eventually leads to wholesale rebuilding, this chapter examines how to prioritize spending on the HR Operating Model, so it continually supports value creation. What investment is foundational and what is discretionary? Putting HR on a "maintenance schedule" that is efficiently tethered to planning routines imbedded in the business is the key to maintaining an effective HR Operating Model.

Before You Call
A Checklist of What to Look at before Calling the Consultants

Let's face it, more often than one would like, calling the consultants often results in being advised to take actions that you already knew were necessary (but for some reason did not take). This chapter provides a checklist that CEOs and CHROS can refer to, of frequently seen symptoms when something is awry with the HR Operating Model, and what the most common causes are – many of which can be fairly easily corrected, others not.

INTRODUCTION

THE FUTURE OF HR? IT ISN'T WHAT YOU THINK

A lot of talk in HR circles lately has centered on the idea that HR needs to find a way to transform itself in an effort to gain a "seat at the table." Pleas from both inside and outside the function have implored HR to step up its game and undergo a transformation in order to deliver more strategic outcomes and business unit–aligned support.

In many organizations, HR transformation has meant taking an elaborate path to drive down costs and streamline people-related administrative work. In these cases, a successful HR transformation simply resulted in cost reductions but not necessarily quality outcomes. Others have attempted to transform HR in different ways including multiple reorgs, introducing various technology solutions, and even outsourcing parts of HR. At the most extreme end, some companies (often high growth tech companies) have elected to delay the creation of a formal HR function altogether.

Since *Fast Company* magazine first published the article, "Why We Hate HR" back in 2005, HR has been faulted, blamed, and "transformed" in an effort to make the function more relevant. More recently, several *Harvard Business Review (HBR)* articles have attempted to define what HR needs to do to get back on track. Everything from splitting the strategic part of HR from the more administrative part to taking a more holistic approach to help the middle 60% of performers has been proposed as a means for fixing HR. A 2015 *HBR* article by Peter Capelli, "Why We Love to Hate HR…And What HR Can Do About It," outlined steps for what HR should be doing now.[1] But these approaches all still miss the mark.

---

[1] Cappelli, P. (2015). Why We Love to Hate HR…and what HR can do about it. *Harvard Business Review Magazine*, July–August.

The ultimate problem with these recommendations is that they are operating outside of the context of business value. The "transformed" HR function lacks a clear definition of and objective evidence to signify its success. That's why we consider the movement toward HR transformation merely iterative and do not believe that it will ultimately be transformational. Until HR can solve the missing connection between value creation and critical *human capital*, it will continue to fall short.

Who Moved My Table?

The issue is not a seat at the table. The table moved; that's the issue. After all, even in the most "transformed" HR environment, HR is still overly fixated on the role of people as it existed in the industrial age – in service of a company's value drivers, which at the time were primarily manufacturing assets. In our new economy, intellectual capital (IC) is the value driver and, as a result, the talent that produces it rules.

IC drives the market values of companies across all industries – one just needs to look to the IC value at companies like Facebook, LinkedIn, or Google. IC makes up nearly their entire market values. Even for more traditional, nontech companies like Walmart and John Deere, IC comprises more than half their value. Knowledge workers have become the most valuable asset for today's organizations and HR's challenge is a supply shortage and much higher portability than the manufacturing assets of old.

Yet, in spite of the many attempts at structural transformation, HR has not been able to adjust to this new reality. Our own experience and research have led us to assert three primary reasons as to why HR has been limited in its ability to achieve measurable progress toward its own "transformation."

1. *HR is untethered from business value.*
   Unconnected to the consequences of the business's performance, either positive or negative, HR operates in the absence of the same accountability framework within which other business leaders operate. The model that HR operates in hasn't changed since the industrial era – there is virtually no differentiation of HR deliverables among all of an organization's roles. At its core, HR does essentially the same thing for all roles, whether it is filling requisitions, compensating employees, planning for succession, or

managing performance. By failing to link HR strategies to business strategy and value creation for companies in a real, measurable way, HR is hindering its ability to play a genuine role in the success of the organization.

2. *HR is operating under the misguided and dated idea that parity equals fairness.*

   While this philosophy might have worked in a manufacturing-centric era, when talent was not the most important asset, this mindset today can have devastating consequences for a company over time. For companies in high IC industries like pharmaceuticals or technology especially, when resources are limited, they simply cannot be spread as evenly and thinly as possible but rather must be invested wisely and judiciously. The fact is, some individuals are more critical to a business because of the roles they play and the value the company derives from those functions. Historically, HR has been unable or unwilling to shift its mindset to make talent decisions based on this new context.

3. *HR is unable to help senior leaders identify where the most critical roles in the business are, based on the company's vision for the future.*

   HR has lacked the leadership and analytical skills to gain a clear understanding of value creation as it relates to hiring, talent development, and employee retention. Without a data-based mentality for decision-making and forecasting, HR cannot facilitate the discussions that are necessary to drive significant changes or overinvest in areas that are critical to the company's talent strategy. Part of this challenge is that HR professionals themselves tend to be more humanistic than capitalistic – according to findings from The New Talent Management Network, most HR incumbents are in the function because they want to help people.[2] Quite simply, their love for and interest in people typically outweighs their love for and interest in the business.

The bottom line is HR's most urgent challenge for the future is to transform itself by gaining an entirely new skill set. The administrative skills and humanistic attributes of the industrial age are now obsolete. Attention must be paid to learning how to define and lead change that is guided by a deep understanding of the value creation for an organization. If HR is unable to accomplish this, then it is destined to become obsolete as well.

---

[2] New Talent Managers Network, *State of Talent Managers Report*, 2013.

A New HR Model

Our belief is that it's not actually a question of HR transforming itself so much as it is the emergence of a new function that will blend two critical business competencies – HR and Finance. The fact is, many business leaders, especially entrepreneurs and start-up CEOs, have a visceral reaction to the notion of "Human Resources." They will do almost anything to avoid hiring HR people because they equate them with bureaucratic minutiae and administrivia. Netflix, which has been credited with "reinventing" HR by doing away with many traditional HR practices like paid time-off policies and formal performance reviews, is a prime example of a company that has taken this tack.[3]

Yet, these same business leaders clearly recognize the importance of talent to their success. Their resistance to HR is due to the perceived administrative burden, rather than the ultimate value they place on taking care of their top talent. At some point in an organization's growth, however, it becomes necessary to assemble some type of HR team. It seems evident that a new breed of human capital professionals is required to ensure that a measurable talent strategy can be developed that truly reflects a deep understanding of the connection between talent and the company's value creation.

In a manufacturing-based economy where tangible capital was the primary means of value creation and the largest expenditure, a close connection between Operations and Finance was required in order to fund and execute economically sound business decisions. Today, Finance and HR need to build an equivalent relationship since human capital is now the primary means of value creation as well as the largest expenditure in our new economy. This relationship will enable companies to maximize people-related financial outcomes and measure the results of these efforts.

In order to be successful, the role of CFO and the role of CHRO must evolve to complement each other. These two roles must champion a new way forward that is rooted in an understanding of the impact of IC on market valuations. The demand for human capital as a method for increasing the

---

[3] McCord, P. (2014). How Netflix Reinvented HR. *Harvard Business Review*, January–February.

value of IC, along with a scarcity of talent, underscore the need for a new model for talent management that will maximize a company's relevant IC.

Key Requirements: Strategy, Leadership, Process

As a first step in establishing this new model, companies should hone their focus on human capital by establishing a strategy that:

1. Facilitates agreement among senior leaders about how IC is produced and then designs a strategy that will maximize its creation.
2. Determines where IC exists within the organization and estimates the relative value of each IC component.
3. Compares where the organization currently is to where it needs to be in order to understand the talent implications of the most valuable IC components.
4. Agrees to overinvest in the attraction and retention of talent in critical roles to avoid future gaps.
5. Defines organizational goals that are related to the IC needs of the future.

More than a fine-tuning of the current HR or Finance roles, this approach reflects a completely new model that can break through the outdated frameworks and perceptions of ineffective HR roles and functions. While we refer to this new model as the "IC Strategy Team" in order to illustrate the point, it is less important to focus on having a different organizational structure or a new title than it is to ensure that this function has an understanding of value creation and an ability to master it.

This new IC Strategy Team that we recommend is truly a hybrid of traditional HR and Finance professionals and skills. In addition to focusing on analytics and measurement, this team also will have a deep understanding of the way in which assets are allocated in order to power market value, as well as expertise in how to attract, select, and retain a high-performing, diverse workforce. A melding of the capabilities of both HR and Finance is necessary to produce the appropriate business solution.

After the strategy has been developed and agreed upon by following the steps above, the process that will deliver the targeted results must define activities, technology, people, and measures. Process design discussions and decisions must ensure that the effort is focused on three guiding principles: increasing business value, overinvesting in critical roles, and measuring efforts and results.

Overinvesting in Critical Talent

Talent processes that are led by the IC Strategy Team will look vastly different than the ones managed by a traditional HR team. Under the new model, there is a laser-sharp focus on differentiating between critical and noncritical roles to guide talent investments.

For instance, under the IC Strategy Team approach, talent acquisition processes would more look like this:

- For critical roles, a team of highly skilled and compensated researchers and recruiters would work closely with hiring managers to find, screen, and close the most qualified candidates. This team would rival the strongest search firms in its ability to surgically find and remove talent from other occupations or companies when business needs dictate.

- For harder-to-fill, noncritical roles, a team of highly skilled recruiters would leverage tools and technology to research, target, and sell and win passive candidates.

- The noncritical positions that are considered easy to fill would be supported by junior recruiters who use technology and assessment tools to screen candidates before passing along the most qualified to hiring managers.

To be successful, this differentiated approach must carry over into all talent processes to continuously ensure that high-performing talent is retained in critical roles. Every step that HR takes must support this new philosophy. As a result, a whole host of commonplace HR processes and practices must change since they make little sense in an IC-driven world.

Take the typical onboarding approach at most organizations. Usually, the formal new hire orientation program is required for everyone and unvaried for anyone. Often led by junior HR or administrative team members, these programs typically focus on the completion of necessary paperwork and lectures related to complying with workplace rules. For a company that has just invested untold resources to entice a top performer to join its ranks, this can be a potentially disastrous first introduction to the organization.

From management training to succession planning and from compensation policies to standard employee engagement surveys, the typical HR approach of parity and equity is dangerously antiquated. Although it may be a bitter pill for HR to swallow, the overinvestment in critical talent is an essential strategy for enabling the creation of business value. Surely the employees working in Accounts Payable or Legal at organizations like Google or Facebook recognize that the Product Designers and Software Engineers are more critical to the success of the overall business. If a rising tide lifts all boats, then in fact, the logic behind overinvesting in those key roles rather than the noncritical Accounts Payable positions becomes crystal clear.

HR's historical attempt to make things "fair" for employees and mitigate exposure to risk often comes at the expense of successful business outcomes and can have a detrimental impact on the business in the long term. By first charting a path that narrowly targets the best talent approaches for a defined group of critical employees, companies can eventually roll out those practices more broadly across the organization. But the first step must begin with overinvesting in the most critical parts of the business and then moving outward.

Who Will Lead the New Model?

We won't pretend that this change to a differentiated, IC-focused approach will be simple. In fact, it will be a huge challenge for businesses and especially difficult for the traditional HR function. But it is absolutely necessary in order to drive sustainable growth via IC for the future.

Infusing HR with these new skills is a foregone conclusion and in some progressive organizations this has begun, albeit in fits and starts. However, even when the skill set and aptitude of HR is modernized in the ideal way, the process for connecting business strategy with talent capability must still be defined.

Building Business Value through Talent helps business leaders close the gap between "CEO and CHRO," between talent and market value. We use the designations CEO and CHRO both literally and figuratively throughout this book to represent the needed and often missing connection between the business and those responsible for supplying and sustaining its human capital.

This guide aspires to give business executives the framework and language to communicate critical business information to their HR partners in a way that can be translated into accurate human capital requirements. It equally aspires to provide HR partners with the framework and language to ensure they have received the information they need to be expertly acted upon.

1

IMPORTANT INSTRUCTIONS

At the Intersection of Talent and Market Value

Building Business Value through Talent is designed to enable CEOs and CHROs to jointly create and operate a talent function within their businesses that will deliver the essential human capital by effectively connecting talent and business strategies. In doing so, enterprise market value will be directly impacted by talent efforts in a positive way over a sustained period of time. Taking this path to a successful CEO and CHRO partnership is necessary due to the fact that intellectual capital (IC) now accounts for more than 84% of the average firm's market value and is an asset whose only source is people's talent.

Our first order of business in this guide is to define the relationship between talent and market value and provide a means for relating this topic directly to your own business.

Market cap growth in the twenty-first century has evolved to become a function of human capital productivity. As recently as 1980, the difference between book value and market value for the average US corporation was not significant. However, by the year 2000, the average company's market value already exceeded book value by about 75%.[1] This excess value that the market places on the average company's share price is attributable to the

---

[1] Giniat, E., & Libert, B. (2001). *Value Rx: How to make the most of your organization's assets and relationships* (p. 10). New York, NY: Harper Collins.

value of intangible assets, specifically IC in the form of brands, trademarks, patents, and other proprietary inventions and commercial secrets.[2] In fact, a nearly 250% increase to the underlying value of the Dow Jones Industrial Average in just the last 10 years, to a market capitalization of approximately $8.3 trillion, is a testimony to the "age of the knowledge worker." (calculated from Dow Jones (DJIA) Historical Total Market Cap, siblisresearch.com).

The way in which talent drives this increase is specific, as illustrated in the following pages.

Although a complex topic, simply speaking, company valuations are based on the discounted value of expected future cash flows. Every analyst following a company maintains a cash flow model that is constantly updated for news that may materially affect both the company's valuation and, in turn, advice given to investors regarding the fair value of the company's shares (and prospective fair value). Those future cash flows will be driven by the performance of a company's assets (Fig. 1.1). As such, although anticipated cash flow is used to calculate a company's market value, that value is ultimately assigned directly to the underlying assets – both tangible and intangible – as evidenced by *business combination accounting.*[3]

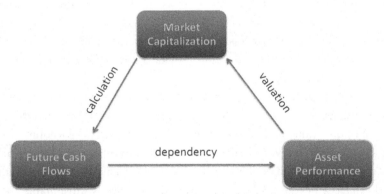

Fig. 1.1.   Business Value Is Based on Future Cash Flow Driven by Asset Performance.

[2] McGuire, T. (2015). *Talent valuation: Accelerate market capitalization through your most important asset* (p. 1), Upper Saddle River, NJ: Pearson Education.
[3] McGuire, T. (2015). *Talent valuation: Accelerate market capitalization through your most important asset*, p. 25.

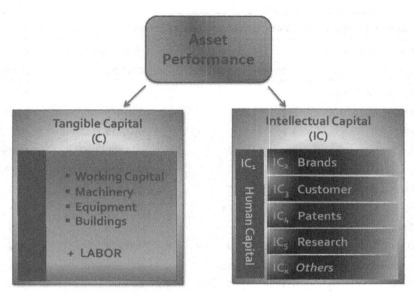

Fig. 1.2. Two Different Types of Assets.

Fig. 1.2 depicts the division of assets between tangible and intangible (intellectual). IC is the focus of *Building Business Value through Talent* because of its dependence on the human capital supplied by an organization's talent. Human capital is a part of IC, and in fact the only "active" component. It is the source of all other IC components, which are by definition "inert." It is the productive capacity of "knowledge workers," a part of the employed workforce. Human capital, the productive capacity of knowledge workers, can be thought of as the means of production for IC.

The actual value split between tangible and intangible assets for your business depends on a number of factors, most importantly the type of industry your business operates in.

To illustrate the relative value of IC for different companies, we use stocks in the Dow Jones Industrial Average. Table 1.1 shows the Intellectual Capital Index (ICI) for the listed companies for the year ended 2019.

In order to avoid confusing users of this information, our data omit oil industry and pure financial services stocks (five companies) in the DJIA. Those companies, which essentially trade the commodities of currency and petroleum, have unique GAAP accounting requirements for significant assets

Table 1.1. The 2019 Talent Growth Advisors Intellectual Capital Index.

Company Name	Rank		Enterprise Value	IC
	2019	2018	($ Millions)	Index
Johnson & Johnson	1	3	396,396	103%
Boeing	2	1	200,675	101%
Microsoft	3	2	962,215	101%
Apple	4	6	948,160	100%
Visa	5	4	348,439	100%
Procter & Gamble	6	7	294,478	99%
Merck	7	11	246,818	97%
Cisco	8	8	218,905	97%
United Technologies	9	9	165,818	96%
UnitedHealth	10	10	311,276	96%
Pfizer	11	5	259,142	95%
Nike	12	12	119,772	94%
3M	13	13	110,304	93%
IBM	14	19	188,801	91%
Home Depot	15	14	277,130	91%
Coca-Cola	16	15	268,486	90%
McDonald's	17	16	180,636	88%
Disney	18	20	277,749	87%
Walgreens	19	17	61,628	80%
Intel	20	21	281,018	77%
Wal-Mart	21	22	364,422	75%
Dow, Inc	22	new in 2019	55,179	71%
Caterpillar	23	23	110,597	67%
Verizon	24	24	362,784	62%
American Express	25	25	141,200	58%

and liabilities (oil reserves and financial capital reserves) that distort financial statements relative to other industries. As "commodity" businesses their value is not driven by IC in the same way as the other 25 DJIA companies.

The ICI is roughly the percentage of enterprise value (market value adjusted to be "debt free") that is represented by intangible asset values based on analysis of year-end financials and financial information. All of these companies' enterprise value is predominantly – some of them entirely – comprised of *intellectual properties* including technologies, processes, patents, and market-dominating brands. Even Walmart and Caterpillar which belong to tangible asset intensive industries have very significant intangible value due to their market leading practices which include customer service and innovation and are reflected in their industry-leading brand positions.

The average percentage of IC value for companies in the 2019 ICI study for DJIA stocks has increased to nearly 89% of market value, up from nearly 86% in 2015, continuing the upward trend.

The methodology for calculating the ICI, which can be done for any public or private company as long as the data are available, resolves accounting anomalies that result in inconsistent ways of dealing with *intangible assets* in regular financial statements.

The first step is to calculate the difference between a debt-free market value (enterprise value) and a debt-free shareholders' equity (book value) of the selected company. Market value for a public company is a calculation of shares issued and outstanding times the market price per share. Net debt is added to that number and to shareholders' equity from the 10-K to calculate *enterprise value* and *book value*.

The difference between enterprise value and book value is the first cut at the value of unrecorded intangible assets in the form of IC (with some exceptions to this rule such as oil reserves of energy companies). These are the assets that are not deemed measurable or certain enough by accounting standards to be included on the books of the company. Yet for investors, these assets are a solid bet, as evidenced by the volume of shares purchased at market value of their owners (think Disney, Coca-Cola, Procter & Gamble, and Pfizer).

Next, goodwill and intangible assets appearing on the company's financial statements as a result of prior acquisitions are identified. We add these components to the unrecorded intangible assets previously calculated to yield the value of total IC. As an example, in the case of Procter & Gamble, the value of the brands Gillette (acquired) and Tide (unrecorded) are in effect being added together as part of calculation of comparable total IC.

IC is entirely the result of *talent*, as is demonstrated in this guide. An important thing to note is that the value of IC includes the value the market places on an entity's human capital and can be accurately and objectively calculated for publicly traded companies (and with the right data, for nonpublic companies as well).

To summarize, the following algorithm is used to calculate what is deemed to be the ICI for a company:

Book Value:
Shareholders' Equity + Net Debt (that is, Debt − Cash and Marketable Securities)
Enterprise Value:
[Market Share Price × Shares Issued and Outstanding] + Net Debt
Intellectual Capital:
Intangible Assets (on books) + Goodwill + [Enterprise Value − Book Value]
Intellectual Capital Index:
Intellectual Capital ÷ Enterprise Value

The high levels of IC value are not confined to only the elite stocks in the DJIA that we've just discussed. IC value for the average public corporation today (S&P 500) exceeds 84%. What is the "means of production" for the majority of this enterprise value? People and their human capital. Yes, people are literally, not just figuratively, the most important asset of many companies across many industries in today's knowledge-driven economy.

This logic of connecting people with value should, once and for all, cast aside the notion that referring to employees as "assets" or "human capital" is derogatory or demeaning. In fact, it's just the opposite and, only when recognized as such, can organizations truly deploy talent in the way they have historically deployed other valuable assets.

Effective talent strategy design and execution is essential to building and sustaining business value because of the way human capital continuously creates and sustains the intellectual assets that in turn drive cash flow. As the "active" component of IC, human capital is dynamic, and the value of intellectual assets is accumulated over time through repeated human capital contributions (Fig. 1.3).

As an example of how this production of IC and market value come to life, we'll illustrate the pharmaceutical company Merck, from our list of DJIA stocks.

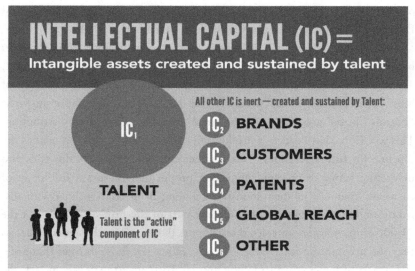

Fig. 1.3. Intellectual Capital (IC) = Intangible Assets Created and Sustained by Talent.

Like other companies in the pharmaceutical industry, Merck's value is almost entirely comprised of IC – most notably in its research and development prowess. Fig. 1.4 depicts a high-level breakdown of Merck's IC based

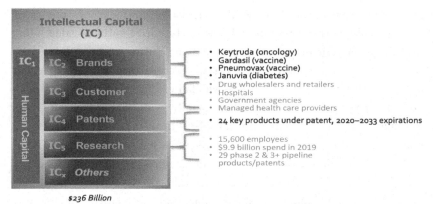

Fig. 1.4. Intellectual Capital Under the Microscope: Merck & Co., Inc.
Source: **2019 Merck & Co., 10K, selected illustrative data.**

on information reported in their form 10K filed with the Securities and Exchange Commission for the year ending December 31, 2019.

We calculated Merck's IC to have a market value of approximately $236 billion. About 22% of Merck's 71,000 employees are in its R&D function. This R&D workforce is responsible for developing and fielding dozens of blockbuster pharmaceutical products over the years including those shown as "brands" in the graphic – fully patented products with global distribution. This workforce has dozens of products in earlier stages of development as the pipeline for future revenues. This product competence allows the sales and marketing teams to present compelling propositions across a full array of customer channels in their industry, building deep relationships with distributors that constitute another distinct part of the firm's IC. Many of the 71,000 employees are in roles that support the drivers of business value, so they too are important to overall success. However, those in roles that are a direct part of the nearly $10 billion annual R&D investment are, in fact, the drivers.

The strategy to build business value through talent must have these "driver roles" in its bullseye – targeting how talent for these roles is most effectively identified, attracted, selected, hired, engaged, and developed. Successfully (and sustainably) attracting and retaining top talent in critical roles will, in turn, yield effective talent practices that will benefit talent across the entire organization.

The essential building block to this approach is understanding which roles in the organization produce which outcomes. The focus of your talent strategy will revolve around the roles deemed to drive business value. While many roles in your organization may support driving business value, typically, only some are considered "critical" because they actually drive that outcome. Also, typically, critical roles will fall within specific functional areas and cluster vertically (rather than horizontally) within the organization. For example, a vertical of researchers (entry-level through leader of leaders) in a pharmaceutical organization would represent such a cluster.

Fig. 2.4 (later in the book) demonstrates a simple model that can be used to categorize roles in your organization according to the degree to which they drive (or support) building business value, and the relative availability of qualified talent in the marketplace to fill those roles. Talent strategy is built around the categorization of these roles into four quadrants. Determining which roles drive and which support business value is a critical point in talent strategy where the CEO, along with his/her management team, must lead the discovery effort – supported by the CHRO. This is precisely where business strategy intersects with talent strategy.

The challenge that your talent strategy must take on first and foremost is the bottom right-hand quadrant – Box 1 talent for roles that drive business value and are in short supply. Not effectively attracting and retaining talent for roles in this quadrant is a "game over" scenario. This is literally where your war for talent is fought.

ALGORITHM IN ACTION: USING INTELLECTUAL CAPITAL TO EVALUATE COMPANIES

To finalize our introduction to the topic of *Building Business Value through Talent,* we'll share some examples of insights we derived from an analysis of select Fortune 500 companies in our earlier book, *Talent Valuation: Accelerate Market Capitalization through Your Most Important Asset* (2015).

Using the IC algorithm further analysis can determine and compare the proportion of IC value to total enterprise value. Calculating this correlation is important because:

- It provides an objective measure of the value of IC relative to total market value on an apples to apples basis, when comparing to other companies.

- It puts into perspective a company's reliance on intellectual versus tangible capital, and as such, can inform talent strategies.

- It demonstrates that building talent strategies based on this analysis, and evaluating them over time, is the most effective way to competitively grow shareholder value for the majority of companies.

- It provides strategic insight into value creation gaps and opportunities compared to a company's competitors.

It is important to note that a higher or lower IC percentage does not mean one company is more successful or more valuable than another, particularly when they are not in the same industry. But what a high IC percentage *does* indicate is that the company has a higher dependence on talent for sustaining and growing market value relative to other organizations. Although the highest IC percentage industries tend to be the more predictable ones – consumer products, technology, and pharmaceuticals – there are notable exceptions, including companies like UPS, Walmart, and Conagra, which have been valued more for their IC than their tangible assets.

A few trends that stood out in our earlier analysis of the Fortune 500 sampling and help demonstrate the dynamics of IC are the following:

- IC Levels Vary by Industry Characteristics
  It is pretty intuitive that a technology company such as Amazon would have most of its value wrapped up in IC – 95% of the company's enterprise value was IC at the time of our analysis. And, pharmaceuticals like Merck & Co. were also driven by IC – 88% of Merck's value was in IC.

  On the flipside, commodity businesses do not survive on IC. For example, Archer-Daniels-Midland (ADM), one of the world's largest processors of oilseeds, corn, wheat, cocoa, and other agricultural commodities, operates in a high-volume, low-margin industry. While it is a solid, well-run business, it does not rely on IC to generate shareholder value. In fact, although ADM ranked higher on the Fortune list (which ranks by revenues) than Amazon, Merck, and Microsoft at the time, it invested just $28 million in research and development in 2012, compared to Merck's $8.6 billion investment. With its more than two dozen active patents and many more products at varying stages of development, it stood to reason that a large percentage (88%) of Merck's enterprise value was attributable to IC, while ADM's stood at only 2%.

- IC Can Help Analyze Companies Within Industries
  Comparing players within the same industry is perhaps one of the most valuable and relevant aspects of the IC analysis. Take Walmart and Target, as just one example. In the pre-recession year of 2006, Walmart's IC percentage was 69% as calculated by our algorithm, compared to a similar IC of 60% for Target. By 2013, however, while Walmart essentially maintained the relative value of its IC at 62%, Target suffered significant depletion to only 40%.

  What happened? Even before Target's CEO resigned in May 2014, there had been ongoing concern among analysts and the media regarding

Target's business strategy. In some circles, it was felt that the corporation had lost its way. In addition, Target took heat for what some perceived as an ineffective expansion into Canada and was criticized for merchandising that seemed to turn away from its core customer. As a result, the market recognized that Target's IC value had declined over the previous 10 years.

- IC Can Help Analyze Individual Companies Over Time
An IC value analysis also provides insight into a specific company's movement over time. In addition to the Walmart and Target comparison, the Coca-Cola Company offers an interesting example to view over time. As of 2012, Coke had an IC percentage of about 84%, reflecting its world-famous brands as well as other forms of IC (unique franchise system, global reach, strategic customer partnerships, etc.) This was down from 89% prior to the company's acquisition of the North America bottling business from Coca-Cola Enterprises (CCE) in 2010. Due to its more tangible, asset-intensive operations, the bottling business actually lowered the relative percentage of IC value to total enterprise value for Coca-Cola.

While this result isn't necessarily good or bad, in the long run, it paints a different picture from an investor's standpoint in terms of how the enterprise value will grow and at what rate. In the case of Coke, acquiring and selling bottling operations is one method of continuously evolving and upgrading the entire system.

By applying the IC algorithm to today's organizations, and competitors, you can gain a deeper understanding of the long-term potential for any given company. Over the past few decades, the growth in the value of the average company has been mostly attributable to intangible value, such as new technologies, brands, and patents. As highlighted above, many different industries have significant IC value and the opportunity for growth in coming years. For a company that hopes to grow in value through IC over the long haul, there must be a concerted effort to hire quality talent and provide support for their contributions.[4]

---

[4] Talent Growth Advisors. (2015). Using intellectual capital to valuate companies: Algorithm in action. Retrieved from https://talentgrowthadvisors.com/resources/blog/using-intellectual-capital-to-valuate-companies.

2

FEATURES AT A GLANCE

Strategic Talent Function and Tools

The role of HR in guiding and supporting the organization's talent strategy is manifold and over time can be measured in terms of the impact it has on a company's market value. In a nutshell, HR actively assists organizations in assessing and addressing talent needs in these ways:

- Planning the workforce

- Marketing employment opportunities

- Identifying and acquiring talent

- Developing talent

- Managing performance

- Compensating and rewarding

All of these can be done tactically, or they can be performed strategically (the formula for *Building Business Value through Talent*). Historically, how these HR activities are executed across the employee population has often been indistinguishable (i.e., tactical) with the exception of perhaps differentiating between hourly and salaried employees while giving separate and unique attention to executives. The essentially one-size-fits-all, tactical, approach earned HR the reputation as a "cost center" – a unit whose allotted spending is spread evenly and nonjudgmentally across the organization; an internal service, with internal customers to serve. Throughout this manual we describe how to make changes that will allow HR spending to become a bona fide investment in the organization's future value.

Fig. 2.1 depicts the typical scope of activities related to delivering talent for the Human Resources function in most organizations, each of which are highly dependent on one another. A modern perspective on the features of each of these activities follows the chart.

WORKFORCE PLANNING

Also referred to as human capital planning, workforce planning (WFP) has the distinction of often being singled out as the most essential, yet least well-performed activity of HR functions by HR practitioners.[1] Why is that? Of all the HR activities, WFP requires the integration of company strategy, plans, functional priorities, and current skills available within the organization. To attempt such an effort across a large, complex business is a challenging effort even with great business acumen and access to necessary data and stake-holders. Typically, all of these elements are outside the scope of the average HR function. Prior to the rise of true human capital in the workforce as the driver of value, the planning function at best was a matter of forecasting labor demand (hours) and projecting fairly straightforward numbers of workers.

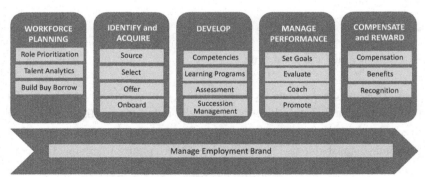

Fig. 2.1. Human Resource Talent Management Activities.

---

[1] Whitepaper – Talent Planning: A Top Priority in the CHRO Playbook. Retrieved from talentgrowthadvisors.com

Today, WFP must be a joint venture between the CEO and CHRO rather than an isolated HR exercise. This is the most critical point in connecting business value with talent. CHROs cannot reasonably be expected to have the same level of insight and understanding of the business strategy and plans as the CEO – however, the CHRO must be highly skilled in receiving that information and accurately translating it into implications for talent. In this regard, it is incumbent upon the CEO to provide the same level of input, direction, and expectations to HR as is normally the case to other key functions like Finance, IT, Supply Chain, and R&D. With this dynamic, the HR function will evolve and significantly upskill to deliver what the business requires. The CHRO and HR function has to successfully receive, translate, and clarify business strategy to be able to accurately answer the following questions:

1. What are the talent implications of our business strategy?

2. What emerging skill sets are in focus?

3. What is the state of our current talent vis-à-vis those implications?

4. What will our specific talent needs and priorities be in the future – by role, functional area, location, etc.?

5. What is the plan for acquiring talent to close gaps – "build" (develop from within), "borrow" (leverage *contingent workers*), and "buy" (acquire talent in a traditional sense)?

6. As a company, which do we currently do well (build, borrow, buy)?

7. What will we need to do well in the future (two, five, ten years from now)? How will we shore up any gaps in our ability to build, borrow, and buy?

8. What are our measures of progress and how will we capture and utilize and improve upon them?[2]

Of course, the ball is in the court of HR to have the requisite tools, skills, and knowledge to accurately answer those questions. Fig. 2.2 shows the full

---

[2] Talent Growth Advisors. (2013). Where Is the ROI for Talent Management? Retrieved from https://talentgrowthadvisors.com/resources/talent-management-roi

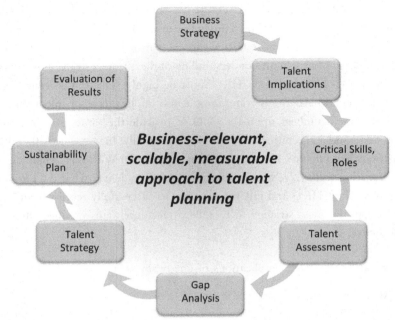

Fig. 2.2. Business-relevant, Scalable, Measurable Approach to Talent Planning.

cycle of translation, analysis, inquiry, and strategy development, as well as measurement, to complete effective WFP.

Planning is truly the only way to optimize the execution of HR strategies. Take for example, recruiting. The optimal recruiting result – finding the best quality hire, on time, in line with diversity objectives, and at the right cost – is not reasonably achievable without planning (Fig. 2.3).

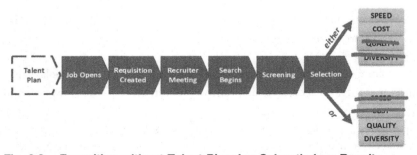

Fig. 2.3. Recruiting without Talent Planning Suboptimizes Results.

As a practical matter, as depicted in the illustration, only the most urgent priorities can be met by a hiring transaction without the benefit of planning – tradeoffs must be made. With WFP, particularly for the most critical roles, hiring can be optimized to meet all requirements, given the appropriate investment in hiring capabilities. The same holds true for development and all other efforts to build and retain talent.

WFP is the lynchpin that connects all other HR activities and informs their priorities. The effort put into WFP should be proportionately more for roles that, by design, create more value and for which talent is in shorter supply. Some support roles with high talent availability do not require much more planning effort than just estimating numbers. Hence, an important sub-activity is prioritizing roles in the organization, using the Talent Strategy Matrix as a framework – the result of this exercise is often similar for businesses within the same industry. The Talent Strategy Matrix plots roles in the organization along the axis of talent availability, and the degree to which the role supports or drives business value. For example, in the tech industry Software Development Engineer (SDE) is likely a Box 1 role (relatively low availability and drives value), whereas Customer Service Rep would be a Box 4 role (Fig. 2.4).

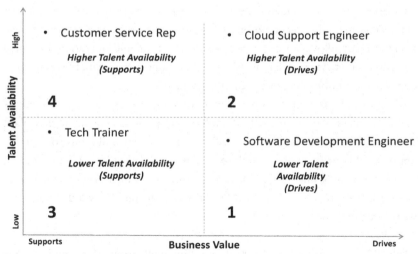

Fig. 2.4.   Talent Strategy Matrix (Tech Industry Example).

We will go into additional detail on making the Build, Buy, Borrow decision in the next section of this manual, but these are key WFP outcomes for each quadrant of the matrix. Here is how we define the terminology:

- *Build* – Developing and retaining talent already employed by the company

- *Buy* – Hiring talent from outside the company

- *Borrow* – Engaging external talent on a temporary basis

When considering each of these options, it's important to weigh the organization's administrative and programmatic capabilities first to assess their likelihood for success. After all, each has distinct requirements to be effectively executed.

For example, for *build* to be a viable primary choice for an organization, the expertise and infrastructure to develop talent must exist. If this is not the case, then it must first be established, and that has to be factored into the timeline and budget equation. Building talent under any circumstances requires time, discipline, and investment. The result can be highly effective, but it might not be a practical solution for immediate needs or for organizations that don't have a track record of building critical talent from within.[3]

In reality, these choices interact with one another at different points in time. As an example, to build talent, it's necessary to have hired that talent in the first place. You may also decide to buy talent that was previously borrowed. The talent strategy allows an organization to orchestrate and operationalize these choices to satisfy talent needs as they arise. Without such a plan, the build, buy, and borrow options default to reactionary tactics.

Talent analytics is an essential element of WFP. For example, your analysis of the business plan for growth, the talent implications created by that plan, and your own internal capabilities will indicate the best build, buy, or borrow approach. Likewise, analyses of the external marketplace supply and demand, of the company's turnover track record, and of compensation trends, especially for critical roles, all provide insight to help build a valid, executable workforce plan.

---

[3] Talent Growth Advisors. (2018). Build, Buy, or Borrow? Determining Your Talent Strategy Game Plan. Retrieved from https://talentgrowthadvisors.com/resources/blog/build-buy-or-borrow-determining-your-talent-strategy-game-plan

IDENTIFY AND ACQUIRE

Talent acquisition is arguably the most important activity carried out by HR due to the downstream, long-term impact of its results. It is not difficult to point to both positive and negative outcomes of talent acquisition activities in major organizations even decades later. Well-executed, strategic hiring has fueled pipelines of talent that ultimately become the leadership team of some companies. In other cases, suboptimal hiring results are a drag on financial resources for years and result in having to repeatedly hire senior leaders from outside of the organization.

Given that resources to invest in hiring are never unlimited, choices must be made: efficiency versus effectiveness. Again, we lean on the Talent Strategy Matrix to guide our decision-making. Box 1 is purely about effectiveness. No wrong hires, no cut corners. This is not to say that money is no object, but it is not the object. Box 1 talent hired successfully will always return the investment many times over.

Box 4 is purely about efficiency. The objective is still to make good hires, but these are supporting roles and talent is relatively available for them. A solid "B" or "C" player in these roles is likely sufficient. These roles will not measurably increase market value; conversely, less than stellar talent hired into Box 1 roles may in fact decrease market value. Again, WFP will indicate the way to invest and organize talent acquisition resources to optimize business results.

An example of how these choices play out for our "tech" company will illuminate these points.

To find a sufficient number of candidates to meet the continuous talent demand for the SDE role in our high-growth tech company, we will need to build and maintain a pipeline of prospects. Once the size and timing of the pipeline is determined through WFP, we can determine the capacity to support Box 1 needs. To successfully manage Box 1 recruiting, we'll need the following Talent Acquisition roles:

- Talent Acquisition Researcher

- Talent Acquisition Sourcer

- Senior Recruiter

The Talent Acquisition Researcher is responsible for identifying qualified leads for the SDE role. Because talent for this role is generally passive (not looking for a job), the Researcher must have sufficient knowledge of the industry along with the technical skills to dig deep into the competitive space, mapping talent in other organizations, following professional associations, and generally infiltrating the industry in search of qualified leads. These leads are then delivered into the pipelining process with full contact information and handed over to the Talent Acquisition Sourcer.

The Talent Acquisiton Sourcer is responsible for converting leads into qualified applicants. A combination of saleperson and psychologist, the Sourcer makes effective contact with qualified leads, piques their interest in the opportunity, listens closely to the goals and motivations of potential applicants, and mentally matches them with specific hiring opportunities and managers. They are expert at determining talent readiness and qualifying leads accordingly. They play a key role in maintaining the depth and quality of the pipeline to ensure a supply that meets business needs.

Directly interfacing with hiring managers, the Senior Recruiter plays a uniquely strategic role in the identification, engagement, and conversion of talent for the SDE role. The Senior Recruiter works closely with the Researcher, the Sourcer, and the hiring team to design and execute talent acquisition strategies for SDE talent.

The Client Lead serves as a talent consultant and advisor to hiring managers, and working closely with the TA team (e.g., Researcher, Sourcer, etc.), selecting talent for SDE roles. Key to delivering these results is the ability to demonstrate business acumen and a deep understanding of the business unit's talent plans; passive candidate conversion and management skills; the ability to screen and select talent; influencing and negotiation skills among a variety of stakeholders (e.g., candidates, hiring managers, etc.); and the ability to convert passive to active candidates through a highly engaged approach.

A Box 4 role within the same tech company would be resourced differently. Using our Customer Service Rep as an example, the entire end-to-end recruitment effort may be performed by a traditional, Full Life Cycle Recruiter.

A Full Life Cycle Recruiter is responsible for managing the experience of the hiring manager, the candidate, and the interviewing team and focuses on roles for which there is ample talent available in the marketplace, such as the Customer Service Rep. The role works closely with the hiring team to screen and select talent for high talent availability roles that *support* the growth of business value.

This recruiter guides leaders through the intake/planning meeting and the entirety of the talent acquisition process. The role involves screening candidates who've applied to active postings and ensuring that candidates who are passed on to interviewing teams meet the hiring standards set by the hiring manager.

In the end, the requirements for identifying and acquiring the right talent for Box 1 critical roles result in a cost per hire that may be 3X the cost for Box 4 talent – effectiveness versus efficiency – impelled by the relative value these roles create for the business.

DEVELOP

The build strategy depends on an organization's capability to develop and retain great talent. Development is not inexpensive and requires real strategy and discipline to ultimately be considered a worthwhile investment and not merely a cost of doing business. Clearly, development spending levels and effort must follow the same type of talent prioritization as seen with Identifying and Acquiring talent.

In addition to technical and institutional knowledge, a cornerstone of development is the competencies that enable an organization's talent to deliver results within the context of the company's business and culture. Knowledge workers are employed to deliver results rather than to perform predetermined tasks, the latter of which is the domain of industrial labor (Fig. 2.5). These

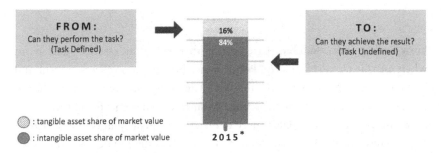

Source: *Intangible Asset Market Value Study 2017, S&P 500, Ocean Tomo®.

Fig. 2.5.   Focus on Managing Talent in Knowledge Economy.

competencies, when exhibited, are the behaviors that optimize performance results over the long haul. Learning to accurately assess for behaviors that indicate key competencies – collaborating within teams, communicating effectively, focusing on customers – enables companies to predict an individual's likelihood to succeed. The HR team leads the identification of appropriate competencies and assesses talent to ascertain strengths and gaps to guide further development.

Talent for critical roles typically merit and require meaningful development efforts. In some industries, such as missile technology, the time that it takes to bring a new hire up to full speed – a missile engineer, for example – can take 7–8 years. These are significant investments.

As another example, consider the role of a Merchant at The Home Depot. Merchants determine the types and quantities of products carried within The Home Depot's retail and online stores. As a relatively small team within the organization, they are responsible for billions of dollars of buys and ultimately determine the success of product availability and sales. They must demonstrate a blend of financial and strategic expertise, a deep understanding of the marketplace, and the ability to negotiate and influence vendors and other critical stakeholders. In that function, external hires are brought in as Associate Merchants and, over time, are trained and developed into the Merchant role. From there, top performers are selected to be Department Merchandising Managers and, ultimately, Merchandising Vice Presidents. These are critical roles for The Home Depot and merit significant development investment which includes assessment, training, and succession in order to ensure internal talent is moved in the most appropriate way.

MANAGE PERFORMANCE

How well an individual has performed in their role is an essential data point when measuring talent quality. Performance information reflects current and historic productivity. We know that well-run companies have approaches to performance measurement that range from traditional and formal to avant-garde or crowdsourced. Ultimately a variety of talent quality measurement approaches can work as long as they accurately differentiate performance.

In recent years, controversial approaches to performance management by some well-known companies have sparked a national dialogue among HR professionals about the value of performance reviews and ratings and subsequent decisions related to pay and promotions. In the last decade, organizations have "eliminated" performance appraisals in an attempt to discontinue what was seen as a laborious and largely ineffective performance management process.

Looking at what organizations are reported to have implemented, we can see some very clear patterns emerging which are likely to form the basis of performance management for a large number of organizations in coming years. These trends are as follows:

- Regular one-to-one performance conversations or "check-ins" initiated by the employee.

- Frequent, in-the-moment feedback from peers and managers, both positive and constructive.

- Near-term objectives rather than annual objectives. Setting and reviewing objectives regularly rather than once a year.

- Forward-looking performance reviews focusing more on development and coaching and less on assessment.

- Fewer or no* performance ratings.[4]

Despite having abandoned formal performance reviews, Netflix somehow strictly assesses talent performance if it is true, as quoted in *Harvard Business Review (HBR)*, that "adequate performance gets a generous severance package."[5] In the same *HBR* article, the author goes on to quote Netflix further: "In many functions – sales, engineering, product development – it's fairly obvious how well people are doing. As companies develop better analytics to measure performance, this becomes even truer." How this type of analysis and assessment of individual performance at Netflix is shared with

---

* Eliminating performance ratings may in fact be a misnomer. Reports indicate that in organizations which "eliminated ratings" they in fact became less transparent but nonetheless existent.

[4] Clear Review. (2019). Performance Management Case Studies: Revolutionaries and Trail Blazers. Retrieved from https://www.clearreview.com/top-5-performance-management-case-studies/

[5] McCord P. (2014). How Netflix Reinvented HR. Harvard Business Review, January – February.

employees is unclear. But in any event, there are undoubtedly years of process improvement ahead for defining and measuring performance, particularly for *knowledge workers*.

COMPENSATE AND REWARD

The cost of compensating and providing benefits to employees is typically the largest single expense on the income statement. Compensation can be a very complex area, especially in large and diversified companies with a large mix of hourly and salaried, seasonal, and other employment variations. Traditionally, events throughout the employment life cycle have triggered compensation decisions – hiring, promotions, annual increases, and even lateral moves. There are salary bands, hourly rates, short and long-term incentives, and the often unfulfilling but necessary benefits.

Some of this is changing. Some of the notable changes in the marketplace are as follows:

- *Annual merit increase*

  After years of struggling with trying to spread 2–3% merit pools over the employee population, irritating as much as motivating recipients, some companies have discontinued the practice. Companies are moving to experiment with market pricing jobs and giving the jobs "fixed" pay rates without the expectation of annual increases. Periodically repricing the market for the jobs can then allow for an inflationary increase (or decrease) to the market pricing.

- *Short-term Incentives*

  Also known as annual bonuses, the short-term incentive has become the singular annual financial recognition above and beyond base pay in a growing number of organizations. Assuming company performance, the annual bonus pool can be large enough to differentiate between levels of performance. It often incorporates, in theory, compensation lost to the discontinuation of annual merit increases.

- *Salary Bands*

    In some cases, organizations add a multiple to market prices for
    select roles deemed to be most critical to companies' performance.
    This may be a boost of 20% or more above the market rate. The
    result is to add a variation to traditional salary bands that differen-
    tiates between all roles and those that are most important to driving
    a particular business' value.

The salary band trend, and the practice of differentiating between roles based
on value contributed, connects directly to the concept of using the afore-
mentioned Talent Strategy Matrix. This framework assists with compensation strategy and decisions and to overinvest in certain roles in order to
maximize business value and returns on investment (Fig. 2.6).

On average, however, it is still a sad truth to say that HR usually has a
better chance of being rewarded more for decreasing the cost of people while
revenue remains flat, than for increasing the cost of people while revenue also
increases, at an even greater rate. Even in a knowledge economy, people as
a resource are by default commoditized through HR practices at most

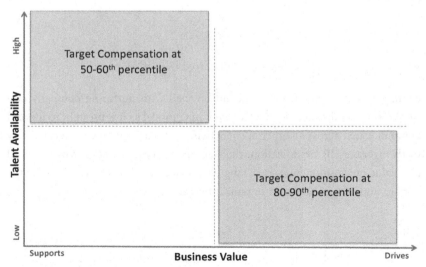

Fig. 2.6.   Talent Strategy Matrix (Compensation).

companies. From defending a 2.0% merit pool, to shaving salary targets from the 70th to the 68th percentile, HR is routinely rewarded for cutting the cost of people in a "defensible" way. That view of compensation is one of cost control rather than value creation.

Will that always be the case? We know that certain talent in every organization produces much more value, by design, than others – and that is beginning to be noticed and acted on more often as noted in "salary bands" above. This differentiation is important and true, not because they are better people, but because the industry and roles they are in and the work they do result in that outcome. Traditional market survey information does not do a good enough job of distinguishing the value of a brand director at a consumer products company from one at a bank, for example. However, the components of intellectual capital that drive market values at those two institutions do in fact differentiate them. Designing compensation strategies to more closely fit the relative value of roles in companies, based on the value they create, will eventually shift the financial view of people from one of cost to one of investment – from one of expense to one of asset. Because human capital is indeed the new means of production, it will require data, appropriate benchmarks, and information systems that can guide this type of optimization.

MANAGE EMPLOYMENT BRAND

Managing the employment brand (intertwined with nurturing company culture) is the broadest activity in HR's operating model as it is brought to life and communicated across all other talent activities. Still in its infancy as a capability of the average HR organization, the state of a company's employment brand and value proposition has a very tangible impact – positive or negative – on the quality and cost of talent an organization can acquire and retain.

Target Audience – The Human Capitalist Investor

In the quest for top talent, an organization's employment brand is the means by which companies position their employment opportunity to the most qualified talent – the "human capitalist investors" – that they most want to attract. These "human capitalist investors," members of the knowledge economy, think about employment the way financial investors think about buying stock. They expect a mix of "capital growth and dividend payout" consistent with their investment goals and risk tolerance. "Capital growth" for the human capitalist means growth in those things that increase their capacity for generating future personal returns. There is an expectation of acquiring certain experience, knowledge, and skills as a result of their investment – that is, employment – decision. A track record of successfully "investing" in reputable companies also adds fuel to their growth potential.

"Dividend payout" for the human capitalist means economic reward in all forms including salary, short- and long-term incentives, and benefits. Clearly for the human capitalist, dividend payout is baseline and must be competitive but will not often win the day on its own. The reason for this is quite rational.

For most of a human capitalist's career, "capital growth" has greater value than "dividend payout" because of its direct impact on future earnings potential. This impact can easily be multiple times current earnings. So, the potential for acquiring knowledge, experience, and skills (and the risk of that not being so) weighs heavily on the employment decision and commitment of today's human capitalists.[6]

This view of capital growth and dividend payout through the eyes of a human capitalist is consistent with a CEB case study in which the top attribute (out of 38) driving both attraction and commitment was "development opportunities," and the top attribute in driving attraction alone was "compensation."[7]

In other words, "I need the right compensation to join, and I need the right development opportunities to join and to stay." Benefits, social responsibility, camaraderie, and a host of other important attributes did not measure up to these most important ones.

In contrast to the bygone prospect of lifetime employment and pension plans, the human capitalist is employed in a world designed for shorter-term

[6] McGuire T. (2015). *Talent valuation: Accelerate market capitalization through your most important asset* (pp. 124–125). Upper Saddle River, NJ: Pearson Education.
[7] Attracting and retaining critical talent segments: Identifying drivers of attraction and commitment in the global labor market. Corporate Executive Board, 2006.

horizons. The trappings of lifetime employment are gone, and today's human capitalist is more likely to "invest" with an expected horizon of three years in mind. In years past it was a red flag to see a resume having three or four different employers within a 12 to 15-year period of time, but the opposite is true today. Today, a 12 to 15-year employment stint can carry with it a stigma of staleness and limited marketable knowledge.

This does not mean that today's relationship will only last three years, but it does mean that the human capitalist routinely reassesses their situation. It is not an announcement but rather a self-assessment of where they stand versus where they expected to be when their investment was initially made. Often, the first assessment occurs somewhere between the two- to three-year mark. What becomes visible are the decisions to pack it in and make a different investment. The decisions to reinvest are not necessarily visible even though they have been made. This same cycle is really no different from that of a financial investor, but it is less visible. Rest assured, every three years or so the human capitalist is likely to re-sign or resign.

These candidates consider alternative investments and compare the potential returns to those of their current investment. Different from the financial investor, to state the obvious, the human capitalist investor as a practical matter can only invest in one company at a time. Ultimately, they make a decision to "invest," keeping in mind the timeframe they are willing to wait before seeing that investment bear fruit. At the end of the day, time is the constraint for this investor... their number of years is limited, so each one counts.

Like financial investors, the intent and strategies of human capitalist investors come in a variety of flavors. You have your short-term and long-term investors, high yield (risk) and growth-oriented investors, and perhaps even an argument for day traders. Which investors do you want? How do you target and attract those investors? Like any corporation raising and retaining financial capital, it is important to have a clear view of who you are and what type of investor best fits your needs.[8]

As you can see, successful employment branding in the knowledge economy looks to be more in the realm of Investor Relations than HR – this is yet another skill set the CHRO's team must acquire. After all, the talent you most want to attract are literally selecting your company because they believe it to

---

[8] McGuire, *Talent valuation: Accelerate market capitalization through your most important asset*, p. 126.

be the best investment of their time and effort. The brand position has to be more fact-based than aspirational. It has to be true, it has to be appealing enough, and it has to express why you are a different and better choice over your competition. The employment brand is a promise that is communicated through every point of contact with potential and existing talent. It extends throughout the employment life cycle. Your talent will expect you to deliver on these brand promises; overpromising and underdelivering will result in more than just bad PR (compare Glassdoor's lowest rated employers list with their employment brands for vivid examples).

The Science Behind Employment Branding

There are countless products and services, case studies, and seminars hawking approaches to building employment branding and employment value propositions (EVPs) – many of which lack the disciplined approach of a formal marketing effort. Unfortunately, companies often prematurely head to the ad agency without having done the strategic work first. The result is an unguided, ineffective tagline or logo and tens of thousands of dollars wasted with unintended market consequences that may leave the company worse off. Advertising conveys a brand and its promises. False advertising is always worse than no advertising at all.

Also note, often employment branding and messaging can be confused (by internal company teams as well as outside consultants) with a company's mainstream product branding. While in some cases the same individual may in fact be in the target audience for both the employment and the product brand, their competitive frame for making those distinct decisions will likely be very different in the two cases (Fig. 2.7).

Having noted that, it is still important for the result of these different branding efforts to have a symbiotic relationship while being distinct and relevant to their goals and target audiences.

Many employment brands and messages attempt to be all things to everyone. They are too broad and nebulous and feature predictable images of a diverse cast of characters. A few do effectively home in on the real target (think about the Marines' campaign targeting potential recruits). Most land somewhere in the vast in-between.

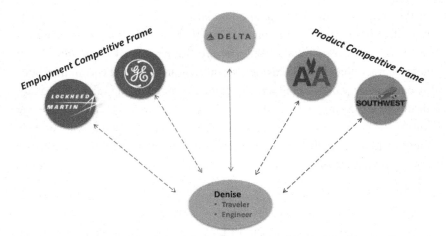

Denise perceives Delta as both a provider of travel services and a potential employer although her competitive frames for those two choices are distinct. A strong EVP addresses the employment competitive frame by zeroing in on drivers of employment choice while remaining harmonious and loyal to the product brand.

Fig. 2.7.   Why a Distinct Employment Value Proposition?

An effective employment brand message should be directed at the heart of the talent most essential to your organization. The following laser-beam approach described in this section accomplishes several things:

- Attracts and retains the most critical talent

- Results in targeted brand promises that have a better chance of being kept

- Has a halo effect on attracting the rest of the organization

- Can be easily adjusted for broader reach

A brand in the true marketing sense of the word has a particular, intentional character and attributes (functional and emotional), all strategically arrived at after very thoughtful research and analysis. A value proposition is technically a way of stating the brand in terms of "what is given and what is received." Obviously, a strong value proposition needs to make a clear and convincing appeal to its target audience for the purpose of being preferred versus other alternatives.

The target audience "bullseye" for an EVP is talent for an organization's most critical roles; those that drive business value (refer to Talent Strategy Matrix).

As depicted by Fig. 2.8, the goals for this EVP are to reach qualified talent, gain consideration and acceptance from the best, and enable an organization to retain selected talent for a sufficient period of time. It goes without saying that the success of even the best EVP is dependent on how it is integrated into and executed within a company's business and employment practices.

The cornerstone of a strong brand position is a few essential and meaningful differences. The temptation to create a list of brand attributes that resembles a buffet must be resisted. An adage used among brand marketers reinforces this point: "If you throw six tennis balls at someone, chances are they will miss all of them. If you throw one, chances are they will catch it."

The branding question is, "What do I have that is important to who I want?" In fact, one option is simply asking those people and getting their feedback. So, assuming the target investor has been well defined, you find a representative sample and gather information from them. These are people who may already be in your organization as well as externals who match the definition. Sources of input from those investors can include:

- Surveys

- Exit interviews

- Recruiter assessments

- Candidate and employee feedback

- Focus groups

- Quantitative research

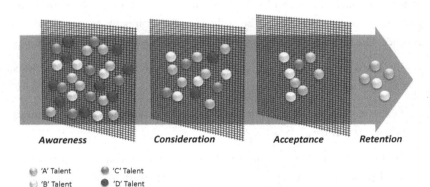

Fig. 2.8.   Strategic Goals for the Employment Value Proposition.

Importantly, the data you are evaluating should pertain to talent for critical roles that closely match your definition of the "ideal human capitalist investor."

It is important to recognize that all 38 employment attributes from the CEB study are valid to some degree and many are even "cost of entry" attributes – you won't get further consideration without them.

Let's assume, for example, your target audience told you the following ten attributes are the most important drivers of choice for them:

- Market position of company

- Organization size and scope

- Senior leadership reputation

- Brand recognition

- Innovation

- Career opportunity

- Compensation

- Retirement benefits

- Social responsibility

- Work–life balance

The next stage of analysis is where the real leverage to brand positioning comes into play. You have identified ten attributes that are most important to your target audience and may be valid for your company to one degree or another. The next step is to identify your true *brand equities* by doing two things:

1. Evaluate how you actually perform in delivering these attributes, i.e., investment advantages.

2. Evaluate your performance in delivering them compared to your primary talent competitors.

As the matrix in Fig. 2.9 shows, there are four outcome categories (and consequences) of these evaluations, as defined further in the following paragraphs.

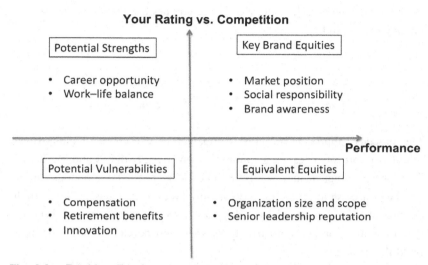

Your Rating vs. Competition

| Potential Strengths |

- Career opportunity
- Work–life balance

| Key Brand Equities |

- Market position
- Social responsibility
- Brand awareness

Performance

| Potential Vulnerabilities |

- Compensation
- Retirement benefits
- Innovation

| Equivalent Equities |

- Organization size and scope
- Senior leadership reputation

Fig. 2.9.   Ranking Employment Brand Advantages.

Potential Vulnerabilities

This category reflects the same low performance by both you and your competition. Although you are judged to be at parity with the competition, you are vulnerable to improvements they choose to make in this important area.

Potential Strengths

Your performance is also not high against attributes in this category, but you outperform the competition. These are potential strengths that can add to the brand and motivate investors while being further strengthened with attention over time.

Equivalent Equities

This category reflects your strong performance while being at parity with the competition. These are attributes that can support the brand position but do not create competitive advantage.

Key Brand Equities

This category reflects strong performance that is significantly higher than the competition. These are the attributes that have the ability to differentiate you in a way that is meaningful to your target audience while being difficult for your

competition to encroach upon. Key brand equities are the backbone of your
employment brand.

Executing an Employment Branding Project

The practical approach for most companies to executing an employment
branding effort is to organize a joint project involving both HR and Marketing.
Each brings complementary skills and knowledge to the table for this cause.

The project is typically broken down into three distinct phases (Fig. 2.10). In
the first phase – the core phase – the work is to define the target audience(s),
determine and conduct informative research, and develop strong insights to
build the value proposition.

Once the EVP is built, the strategy for implementation must be finalized
including steps to coordinate the EVP with other company messaging to other
constituents and completing objectives for the EVP across the employment
life cycle. The 3rd phase activates the EVP and plan via marketing executions
and feedback loops to gauge and adjust effectiveness.

The effectiveness and productivity of the EVP all hinge on the information
and insights that go into producing it. As such, the approach to research in
phase 1 of the work will characterize the final outcomes.

What does all of this end up looking like in real life? Here is a summary level
view of the creative brief, as an example, for the critical role of Product Management in a technology services company (XYZ-Co). The creative brief (for all
you nonmarketers) is a product of the EVP that the developer of marketing
messages and collateral materials – usually an ad or PR agency – work from to
ensure targeted, relevant communication is designed.

EVP Creative Brief
Critical Role: Product Management

Background: XYZ-Co is a technology services leader committed to helping
people get the most out of their technology platform and balance the inter-
dependency between life and technology

Job Function: The Product Management job function is responsible for
leading the product design effort in new market launches as well as for identifying and driving improvements in financial performance, customer experience,
and utilization of in market products. Partner with other product leads from

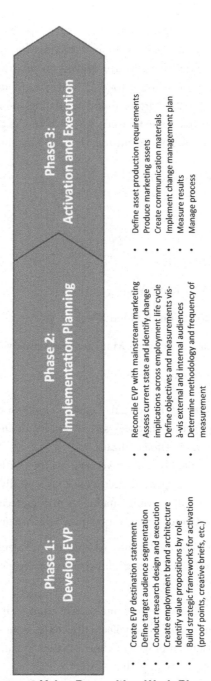

Fig. 2.10.   Employment Value Proposition Work Phases.

multiple product teams to define and sell-in a client specific product roadmap with existing and prospective clients. Individuals are responsible for exceeding client expectations through the effective delivery of programs and initiatives. Jobs in this function are responsible for KPI management and effectively articulating the value of XYZ-Co's products and capabilities, along with identifying new opportunities to drive value between XYZ-Co and its clients.

Priority Motivators of Top Talent for This Job Function:

#1 Opportunities for Advancement

#2 Job Security

#3 High Compensation

#4 Work–Life Balance

#5 Interesting and Challenging Work

#6 Management Recognition of Good Work

#7 Open Communication Between Manager and Employees

#8 Collaborative Workplace

Persona Target Segment: Individuals highly focused on career progression. They are proactive go-getters that seek self-advancement and view their career success as an extension of self-actualization.

Persona Attributes: Highly inquisitive persons; they gather data and information to enhance better designs and decisions. They typically want time to make comparisons and review all relevant data before making recommendations.

Persona Key Traits: Intellectual, Inquisitive, and Patient

The Value Proposition for Product Management Talent (this is not a tag line or verbatim advertising language; however, creative geniuses derive those from this concise statement):

> "If you are an inquisitive and innovative thinker that thrives on change and is motivated by intellectually challenging opportunities, XYZ-Co is the right employment choice as they are an agile and fast paced technology company that fosters career advancement and provides employees the opportunity to disrupt the status quo by enhancing the way people live and giving you a chance to work with innovative technology."

The Creative Brief draws on all the science and analysis described in this employment branding section to deliver a laser focused guide for communicating to the talent that is most important for you to hire and retain. The work can be done at this role or job function level for the most critical talent needs and at an organization level (with less individual focus) for the more general support functions, all delivering the DNA for accurate and effective messaging.

Caution: Chapter 2 Concluding Thoughts – Prerequisites for Installing the HR Operating Model

Before beginning installation of the HR operating model blueprinted in this guide (designed to build business value) it is important to gauge the readiness of the existing HR organization and address the most significant, codependent, issues experienced by other organizations – to the extent that they exist.

HR Capability

Many corporations historically have had few, if any, strategic positions dedicated to HR. When they do exist, they are often hampered by a wide range of administrative burdens related to the processing of people transactions throughout the company. The work result demands are often not financial or analytical in nature because the HR function itself is not positioned as such. Overwhelmed with administrative responsibilities with few demands related to strategy or measurement, these roles are quickly viewed as having low "authority", which causes them to have great difficulty establishing credibility, assessing strategic opportunities, and driving results-based change. This basic capability issue needs to be resolved before proceeding further.

HR Function Mindset

When jobs are tactical in nature, they appeal to people who like tactical work. Many HR professionals, when surveyed, report a preference for administrative, nonstrategic work. They often have a low tolerance for risk and a limited sense of what they care to "own" or have authority over. Other studies have indicated that HR professionals lack confidence in their own skills and abilities, which leads people to choose administrative work over more strategic, analytical career opportunities. Separately, one significant study revealed only 32% of HR leaders have high confidence in their strategy or actions.[9]

The mindset of being a "support function" rather than a driver of business value must be resolved to move forward successfully to installation.

Linking HR Work to ROI

CHROs are too often unable to gather and use data to build business cases that attract confident investment from executive teams in their company's talent strategy. Coming full circle, this is usually the result of HR Capability and Support Function Mindset issues.

To break the cycle and move to installation these three prerequisites should be addressed up front.

[9] Talent Growth Advisors, Where is the ROI for talent management?

3

INSTALLATION

How to Start or Restart the Strategic HR Function

Whether you are a new, rapidly growing business that is ready to invent HR at your company or a fully mature organization that needs to restart how HR works, the key to installing new HR capability is effectively merging what we know about creating market value via intellectual capital (see Chapter 1) with what HR is tasked to do (see Chapter 2) and optimizing the connection. Attaining this strategic insight and acting on it will propel HR from a cost center to an investment vehicle over a relatively short period of time.

What we term a Value-Driven Talent Strategy, when executed, will ensure above all else that the organization always has the right talent in *critical roles* as a business imperative (Fig. 3.1).

The implication of a Value-Driven Talent Strategy is that critical roles require greater investment than most other roles. Contrary to what has historically been practiced in most companies, higher investment means that the way talent for critical roles is recruited, developed, measured, rewarded, and retained should be unique to those roles – they are differentially invested in. The result is a higher return on investment in talent for the company than has been previously experienced because of the direct connection to market value.

What proportion of roles should be considered "critical" in any given organization? The number of critical roles will vary with the size and nature of a company's intellectual capital and the way in which it is produced. An industry whose ICI is typically 90% of enterprise value will likely have proportionately more of their jobs in critical roles, among nonmanufacturing

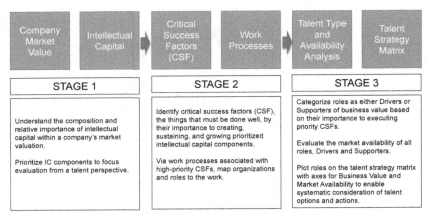

Fig. 3.1.   Value-driven Talent Strategy.

employees, than those with IC at 50% of enterprise value. The absolute number of critical roles in an organization depends on the scale of the company. However, the number or proportion of critical roles is ultimately less important than the method by which they are identified and leveraged. On average we have observed about 20% of the employee population being in critical roles although this can vary greatly across companies and industries.

HR's approach to a value-driven strategy is different from how it has normally approached its work in the past. It begins with differentiating an organization's roles and the consequent talent needs of those roles. The CHRO cannot accomplish this first and most essential step without direction from and partnership with the CEO. In *Building Business Value through Talent*, the CHRO facilitates the executive management team in identifying those roles in the organization that drive business value versus those that support it – this work ultimately determines the mix and deployment of HR resources in an investment model that is directly connected to increasing business value.

In **Stage 1**, the IC Inventory and Analysis essentially replicates the analysis we reviewed earlier for Merck (Fig. 2.1), for your company. Qualified internal HR consultants (which may be a new HR role for an organization) work with the executive team to fashion a picture of the highest value IC components for their company. The mindset for this work should be forward leaning, consistent with what might be shared with prospective investors to motivate their investment decision; what "assets" does the company possess, and intend to possess, to create competitive business value (i.e. drive cash flow)? If the inventory of IC is exhaustive and large, it should then be prioritized to isolate the greatest values and categories to focus on.

Once the highest value IC components are understood, **Stage 2** maps the work done by the organization to create and sustain those components and thereby identify the roles that do the work. Assuming, for example, branding to drive the sale of a product is a high value IC component, doing Consumer Marketing would likely be critical and the work processes that enable this to happen must be very important and lead to roles that are critical within that organization.

Using the Stage 2 process for a well-known brand such as Coca-Cola, we demonstrate at a high level how workflow analysis enables the identification of critical roles (Fig. 3.2).

In this example, the company has estimated the value of brand Coca-Cola to be $80 billion, clearly a significant number relative to an Enterprise Value of $180 billion. Consumer Marketing, along with other brand related factors is critical to successfully building and nurturing the brand. The work of Consumer Marketing includes conducting Marketing Intelligence studies and analysis. This work is determined to be done by Category and Brand Managers. As a result, these roles are now defined as critical (i.e. drivers of business value).

Intellectual Capital Example: Brand Coca-Cola

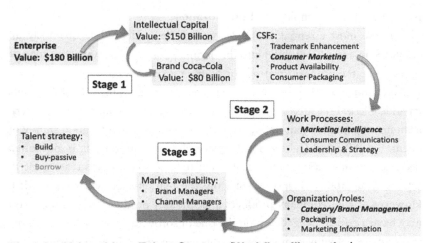

Fig. 3.2. Value-driven Talent Strategy (Workflow Illustration).

In **Stage 3** of the value-driven talent strategy, critical roles that have been identified as driving business value, as well as the other roles in the organization that support those efforts, are further analyzed to determine the extent of talent availability in the marketplace for them. The results of that analysis are mapped to the talent strategy matrix (which was discussed using a Tech Industry example in Chapter 2 of this guide – Fig. 2.4), and following this, strategies for managing the supply of talent in each quadrant of the matrix are built.

The strategic decisions that HR must evaluate and make for each quadrant in the Talent Strategy Matrix include the following:

- Build, buy, borrow choices and prioritization

- Investment in pursuit of passive versus active candidates

- Compensation competitiveness relative to market prices

- Development plans and investment levels

- Focus of attraction and retention approaches and investment levels

By design, each of these decisions depends on the value created by roles in each quadrant and the relative scarcity of talent for them. This dynamic serves to build ROI optimization into the talent plan. A thumbnail description of each choice follows.

Build, buy, borrow choices and prioritization

This is the most essential talent decision to be made. While obviously all employee talent is hired (*buy*) into the organization at some stage, this may or may not be the primary strategy for filling a given role.

An example of when it may be the primary strategy is the role of Accounts Payable Clerk. Like all roles in your organization the Accounts Payable Clerk is an important one – but unlike some roles, there is usually a good supply of talent for AP Clerk in the marketplace. Because of this, it is not often necessary to maintain a pipeline of talent for this role and it's reasonable to rely on your ability to hire talent from the marketplace when it's needed. However, if your company produces a technology product, for example, you may have a critical dependence on the role of software engineer for which the marketplace is highly competitive. In this case merely relying on hiring talent from the external market directly into this role is an unwise strategy – while necessary to be able to do so, a stronger strategy would also include a *build* component and perhaps *borrow* as well.

Build, Buy, Borrow definitions:

Build means developing talent internally, which implies that the organization has the capability to effectively engage, develop, train and retain employees. In terms of career pathing, there are typically multiple position levels for a given role that a person can progress through as they are developed. Build is an important strategy when talent is not readily available and/or when the time to be effective in a particular role is extensive. More targeted retention approaches incorporate a build strategy – such as new graduate hires into a leadership development program. In such a case, it is understood that talent for such leadership roles is not easy to replace and the investment made in development is high.

Buy means hiring directly from the external marketplace. There are multiple sub-strategies for the buy choice which would include considering passive (those not actively looking) in addition to active candidates, and sourcing through more effective channels. These sub-strategies boil down to efficiency versus effectiveness and to level of investment warranted.

Borrow means contracting for non-employee talent, or contingent workers, on a not-permanent basis. Although common for many types of support roles, borrow also applies to critical roles in certain circumstances. Often when new skillsets are breaking into the market (for example, early on with digital marketing and now several popular, but still niche, technology skills) it is nearly impossible and likely unaffordable to actually employ the talent – they can name their price so you have to buy by the shot glass rather than the barrel. Contingent workers have gone mainstream as a source of talent. These *"free agents"* cite work-life balance, schedule flexibility, and work variety as reasons along with ability to earn same or better compensation.

Fig. 3.3 shows an example of what would likely be the categorization of 4 different roles in a technology company.

As you can see in this example, quadrant 1 has a primary strategy to build talent for the Senior Software Engineer role. When executing the secondary strategy, buy, the target is the passive candidate because market demand fully exceeds talent availability. Due to the relative scarcity of ready-now talent

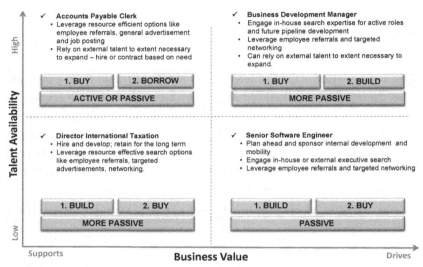

Fig. 3.3.   Talent Strategy Matrix (Technology Company).

and the long learning curve, the Director International Taxation role also will rely primarily on build – the objective is to have promotable internal talent for this role and a strong retention focus.

The Business Development Manager is a role which also drives business value, but the skillset is more readily available in the marketplace than for a Senior Software Engineer. Because of this, Buy is an appropriate strategy for acquiring talent for the role. At the same time, because the role is critical to the organization, Build is a valid second strategy.

While the Accounts Payable Clerk is certainly a necessary supporting role, talent is readily available and replacement, i.e., Buy, is the go-to talent strategy in this example. Borrow, that is utilizing a contractor, is also a useful strategy for this role since the learning curve is not steep and it is a supporting rather than driving role.

The Director International Taxation supports rather than drives business value, but highly qualified talent for these specialty roles is often difficult to find. A number of hard to fill support roles, usually niche-type skillsets, can be found in most organizations and normally require advanced recruiting techniques to acquire. They are well worth the investment to groom internal talent for advancement and to fund retention strategies.

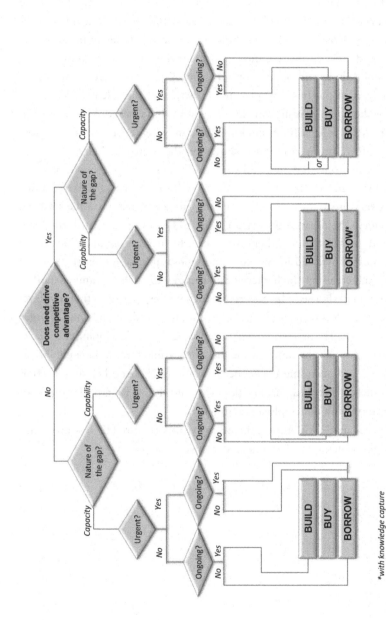

Fig. 3.4. Build, Buy, Borrow Decision Tree.

*with knowledge capture

As we've said, these choices interact with one another at different points in time. To build talent, it's necessary to have hired that talent in the first place. You may decide to buy talent that was previously borrowed. A talent strategy enables an organization to plan for these choices to satisfy talent needs before they arise, and more easily operationalize them when they do. Without such a plan, the build, buy, and borrow options simply become reactive tactics.

An analysis of the business plan for growth and the talent implications created by that plan can inform the best build, buy, or borrow approach. A decision tree that is useful in thinking through which choice would be most appropriate for a given situation is shown on the previous page (Fig. 3.4).

The HR organization design and structure will evolve in step with business strategy and the go-to talent strategies selected to meet business needs over time. These can vary greatly, even within the same industries based on the strategic choices made. One organization may choose to be best in class at hiring new college grads and developing them from scratch; such an organization would likely resemble a pyramid in structure and would ultimately thin the internal talent pool at increasingly higher levels as talent moves up the pyramid. Another organization may choose to be best in class at sourcing and attracting mid-level (experienced) professionals and would have more of a diamond shaped organization structure. The first would build deep capability in developing entry-level professionals through the ranks, while the latter would have built capability at searching for and acquiring experienced professionals. Another organization may be fixated on built-in agility and flexibility and choose to staff a large part of its organization with nonemployee contractors.

The choices made will inform the best way to structure HR resources and support the business plan and talent strategy.

4

CONTROLS

The Most Important Facets of the HR Operating Model and How They Can Be Monitored

The ability to execute HR talent initiatives is pointless without understanding what success looks like for the business and having the means to monitor progress and remediate shortcomings. The ubiquity of data in modern HR systems can easily overwhelm and not effectively aid in making the highest priority decisions and course corrections. By activating the Value-Driven Talent Strategy, a business connected HR operating model (people, process, technology, etc.), enables the talent strategy's execution. This section of the guide identifies the stages of execution and delivery in the HR operating model that are most essential to ensuring successful investment outcomes and which should therefore be closely monitored and measured.

TWO TYPES OF HR METRICS

Two categories of metrics should be thought through and put in place to drive the long-term success of the operating model: *Operating Metrics* and *Results Metrics*. Like many business functions, HR is very process based, especially for the work that relates to acquiring, developing, and sustaining talent.

Operating metrics gauge how well those HR processes are working. By looking at quantitative data that indicate the efficiency and effectiveness of

Throughput

- Volume, Mix (Internal and External), and Type

Process

- Time to Fill by Stage
- Interviews/Hire Ratio
- Candidate Dropout Rate
- Offers Accepted/Rejected
- Cancelled Requisitions

Productivity

- Cost per Hire
- Recruiter (workload, TTF, Fills, etc.)

Operating metrics gauge the efficiency and effectiveness of efforts to produce Results. They are used to evaluate operations, produce actionable information, and course correct as needed.

Fig. 4.1.   Operating Metric Examples (for Hiring Process).

a process, operating metrics provide the information to continuously improve how execution is working. An example of typical operating metrics for the recruiting area are shown in Fig. 4.1. Similar kinds of operating metrics can be captured for other areas of talent management and HR work.

Results metrics, on the other hand, are the "bottom line" (Fig. 4.2). What did the processes produce and how did results compare to expectations and prior experience? Significant variances in results metrics would typically be investigated by following the path back through underlying operating metrics. For example, in recruiting, if the quality of new hires seems inadequate, one might analyze recruiter workloads, candidate generation per requisition, etc., to find what process steps can be adjusted and tracked for their impact on quality.

Goals for an organization are normally measured through results metrics and diagnostics revert to operating metrics and the relevant processes. HR should be no different.

Dozens of operating metrics are important to the overall effort involved in managing talent outcomes. After all, talent management is complex and

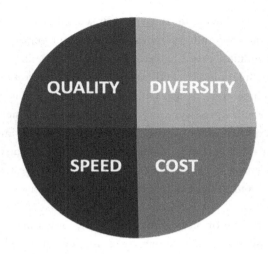

*Results metrics are strategic goals to be prioritized.
Growth organizations producing intellectual capital
prioritize Quality, Speed and Diversity – at best
achievable Cost.*

Fig. 4.2. Results Metrics.

spans the entire employment life cycle, including planning, acquiring, developing, and retaining talent. As with any such effort, there are expectations for effectiveness and efficiency and a need to drive continuous improvement. Looking across the talent management spectrum at activities such as recruitment, development, and compensation, it is obvious there are many subprocesses intended to work together to achieve the overall goals of talent management. At different stages in each of these subprocesses, outputs are produced that are important to measure so information can be provided to improve and optimize the work.

To illustrate this concept, imagine driving a manual shift transmission automobile down a deserted highway. On this highway, the speed limit is marked 70 mph, and signs also note that the minimum speed is 40 mph. If your priority were to drive this stretch of road in an *effective* way (legally!), you would simply stay on the high end of this speed range. If you also wanted results to be *efficient*, you would focus on optimizing fuel usage too and find a balance within that range. But in reality, as you drive your car, there are many subprocesses and operating metrics that have an impact on your ability to maintain speed within the desired range while optimizing fuel usage. Trying to maintain this speed in second gear would send your rpms through the roof and eventually overheat your engine, so a tachometer helps you monitor this. Engine temperature can be impacted by other issues (such as coolant levels), and overheating can stop you in your tracks, so there is a temperature gauge. Oil supply to the engine is essential, and therefore you can keep an eye on your oil level measurement as well. In addition, each of these subprocesses has a target operating range built in as a measurement – a light comes on, literally, when you are outside the range. These and other factors in gauging your car's activity are essential to being able to manage and achieve the effectiveness and efficiency goals that you have set.

As in this example of driving an automobile, measuring talent management subprocesses – such as the time it takes to fill a vacant role or the range of performance review scores – can tell an important story about how efficient and effective we are at managing talent. Without a doubt, there are dozens of subprocess measurements that are important to managing the overall talent process. But the strategic objectives of the entire, connected realm of talent management dictate which are the most essential metrics to monitor and achieve.

In a world where value is driven by knowledge the strategic objectives of the talent process must prioritize talent for Box 1 roles (see Talent Strategy Matrix). They are the drivers of business value and are also always in short supply. But how do we differentiate between the importance of the "oil gauge" and "speedometer" as measurement tools to successfully guide us in managing that talent? The answer lies in understanding their impact on the most important results metric for Box 1 – quality. Why quality, and how can that even be measured?

Knowing Quality When We See It

How can talent quality be observable when one is producing something that is invisible? We turn to a study that was a key source in a case study on talent quality published by the Corporate Executive Board (CEB).[1] The study,

---

[1] Driving quality beyond the point of hire. Corporate Executive Board, 2002. p. 9.

Differences in Output Variability as a Function of Job Complexity, was conducted by university researchers and reported in the *Journal of Applied Psychology*.[2] In this study, the researchers determined that output variability of talent was large and increased significantly with job complexity. The data indicated that output variability in complex, professional roles varied by a factor of 12x between an average performer and the best performers. An excerpt from the study conclusions makes the point succinctly on the challenges and benefits of measuring productivity (output):

> The data presented in this study show that individual differences in output are very large. It is clear that if people could be selected for jobs on the basis of a reliable measure of output, the differences in output between those selected and the average for the applicant pool would be very large...the employer must select on the basis of measures that have been shown to correlate with (and thus predict) future output.

Two main takeaways from the study were these:

- There are large gains in productivity to be made by selecting better workers

- Individual differences in job performance are the key dependent variable

Understanding differences in productivity of knowledge workers is the challenge to understanding quality. By doing so, the creation of intellectual capital (a patent, brand, customer relationship, and so on) and the associated value can be exponentially increased. The best talent is more successful delivering results – they produce more value. How can the productivity of talent – the quality – be measured?

The study referred to above was based on actual observation of work and workers; this is a proof point but not a practical way to manage measurement of talent results on an ongoing basis. Multiple studies and papers have referred to a combination of factors – logically, performance data – and three others that in combination should be utilized to judge legitimate quality.

---

[2] Individual differences in output variability as a function of job complexity. *Journal of Applied Psychology*, 1990.

These four data elements – performance, potential, promotion, and retention – can be used to measure talent quality on an individual level and also be extrapolated on a larger (that is, department or function) scale. Here are descriptions of each factor, why they are important in the mix, and how they can be separately measured:

Performance

No matter how you cut it, how well an individual has performed is the essential data point when measuring talent quality. Performance information reflects current and historic productivity. We know (and described earlier) that well-run companies have a variety of approaches to performance measurement. For the purpose of assessing talent quality, various approaches can work as long as they accurately differentiate performance.

Because individual differences in job performance are so important to identifying more productive workers, it goes without saying that this data point is a key part of the quality equation.

Potential

Estimating potential can be even more powerful than determining performance because it is a future-oriented view of an individual's longer-term productivity. Organizations that currently utilize potential ratings consider factors including past and current performance, capabilities exhibited (including fit within the organization), and the individual's expressed desires. Sometimes, more elaborate methods are used to evaluate potential, such as simulation-based assessment centers.

In many organizations, evaluation of potential takes place among a certain level of employees – typically wide but not deep. Therefore, a particular company may assess the potential ratings of all Vice Presidents and, based on this data, may determine successors for higher level roles. This isn't a bad practice, but organizations should also be identifying successors and gathering data about the bench for all mission-critical roles – Box 1 roles that drive business value. Going deep into verticals with critical roles that drive the most value – even when that includes entry level, yet essential pipeline roles – is worth the time and effort.

Potential in the quality equation, factors in the future, sustainable element inherent to any form of capital.

Promotion

Whereas Potential and even Performance data inherently includes a dose of subjectivity, Promotion and Retention reflect facts. Whether an individual has been promoted within a certain period of time is a tangible data point indicating productivity. Significant pay adjustments that are not technically promotions may also be tangible data points.

Retention

Retention data – simply knowing who remains with the organization and who has left, regardless of the reasons – is essential to assessing talent quality. Productivity always requires a learning curve to reach full potential, whether an entry level or experienced hire. Quality – a reflection of productivity – must include a retention factor to be accurately stated.

Retention data and trends, perhaps more than any other people data, help organizations understand the value of the talent investments and the effectiveness of talent processes. The implication of retention issues, especially among critical talent, can range from gaps in the hiring process to the engagement strategy, onboarding, or even leadership quality.

The use of these four data points allows organizations to apply their best knowledge of historical and future performance, reinforced by tangible recognition, and factoring in sustainability (retention) to produce a solid basis for leveling talent quality.

Talent quality is ultimately defined as sustained productivity. It requires the passage of time to be revealed and observed. In the case of new hires, it takes a significant period of time to settle a person effectively into the organization. Depending on the resources dedicated to achieving a rapid assimilation, a period of at least several quarters is typically required before one can become fully productive. In our experience, 24 months is probably the shortest period of time within which measuring quality data is meaningful. Because of that, we advocate an approach that captures a qualitative snapshot soon after hire via manager feedback as well as structured observations followed by quantitative measurement after the passage of time.

HR data systems now make it relatively easy to begin tracking talent quality using the four data points we described. As with using any data, the integrity of the data itself directly impacts the reliability of information produced from it. Organizations should move firmly to institute practices that refine their performance and potential data; mandating standards and methods for gathering and recording these data are essential.

The combination of performance, potential, promotion, and retention data is best expressed as an index – a measure that can stand alone as an absolute number and be easily compared to prior periods to track the overall change. The index itself should be a data tool that can be easily dissected into slices and provide insight and aid in identifying process and market opportunities for improvement.

Our weighted quality index (WQI) is a 1.0 version of this tool that we have successfully piloted with clients. The WQI defines levels of quality based on combinations of performance, potential, promotion, and retention and is weighted by assigning a productivity factor to each level (Fig. 4.4). A higher productivity factor associated with each higher level of quality yields a weighted calculation of the index. This in turn provides an absolute metric representing quality achieved during a given period of time and provides the means for systematic improvement.

We designated the four quality levels in the WQI as: Superstar, Star, Average, and Below. This model assumes a 4-point scale for rating both performance and potential, a defined set of minimum criteria for reaching each "Quality Level," and the requirement of at least 24 months in the role. The productivity factors assigned to each quality level are based on the CEB case example we have referenced that studied differences in productivity between high and low performance of computer programmers.

Although this may seem arbitrary when related to other roles, it is nonetheless a reliable data source and a legitimate benchmark.

To demonstrate how the WQI works, we use the hypothetical example of 25 people hired into Senior Researcher roles at a pharmaceutical company (Fig. 4.3). After 24 months, these researchers are evaluated based on performance, potential, promotion, and retention. Based on this evaluation, the 25 are categorized by level of quality according to the Superstar, Star, Average, and Below levels. We then rate each by the corresponding productivity factor. A weighted average is calculated for the group by dividing the factors total by the number of individuals. This is the resulting WQI.

As is apparent in the calculation of the WQI, the effect of the productivity factors is to increase the index disproportionately when Star talent or better is present. An organization could choose to use larger or,

PRODUCT DEVELOPMENT SENIOR RESEARCH HIRES QUALITY ANALYSIS — LATEST 24 MONTHS AS OF DECEMBER 31, 2019

NAME	TITLE	DEPT	START	SOURCE	PRIOR JOB	PERFORMANCE	POTENTIAL	PROMOTION	RETENTION	QUALITY RATING	FACTOR
Noma Vanhorn	Senior Researcher	2139	1/2/17	Referral	Honeywell	M	WP	N	Y	A	1
Marianela Abate	Senior Researcher	2574	1/13/17	Internal	Operations	E	P	N	Y	S	3
Steve Spratt	Senior Researcher	3140	2/22/17	Linkedin	P&G	M	WP	N	Y	A	1
Rodrigo Bonnie	Senior Researcher	3140	2/26/17	Linkedin	Raytheon	GE	H	Y	Y	SS	12
					data abbreviated for this example						
Greg Lutz	Senior Researcher	3140	7/13/17	Agency	Djrax	M	WP	N	Y	A	1
Rick Schlict	Senior Researcher	2574	8/20/17	Internal	Regulatory Affairs	E	P	Y	Y	S	3
Helen Nomad	Senior Researcher	2139	9/29/17	Internal	Testing	E	H	N	N	B	–1
										FACTOR TOTAL	55
										WEIGHTED QUALITY INDEX	2.2

Calculating Quality
On basis of productivity ratings

Productivity Rating	Criteria at 24 Months Tenure			
	Performance	Potential	Advancement	Retention
SUPER STAR (12X)	Greatly Exceeds	High	Yes	Yes
STAR (3X)	Exceeds	Promotable	No	Yes
AVERAGE (1X)	Meets	Well Placed	No	Yes
BELOW (-1X)	Not Meet or Exit	Questionable	No	Yes or No

Fig. 4.3. Quality of Hire Indexing and Management.

alternatively, more modest numerical factors for their quality levels and achieve a more or less exaggerated index. What is important is not the absolute value of the index, but rather how the index value compares to other time periods and how it is used to identify opportunities for improving talent quality.

As indicated in Fig. 4.4, using the example of the 25 senior researchers, after "quality" is calculated, we can slice the data many ways, including by type – internal or external – and by source. The analytics are unlimited.

Naturally, the opportunity to begin measuring quality presents itself when a new hire is made, and for similar reasons the same opportunity exists when an internal placement is made. In the case of an internal move when an individual changes role (not a promotion in place), an event is triggered that legitimately resets the counter for quality indicators. In effect, the organization makes a decision to fill a need with an internal resource or an external hire. In a separate study conducted by the CEB, variations in performance of internal transfers were captured that reinforces the wisdom of measuring quality at this juncture. The study captured the frequency with which organizations say they were able to place an "A-level" internal hire (the right person for organization and job, with the right tools needed

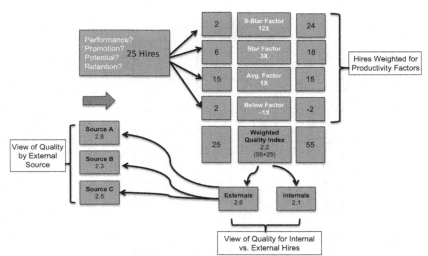

Fig. 4.4.   Example: Measuring Quality of 25 Senior Researcher Hires (Internal and External Hires at 24 Months in Role).

to do the job). Out of 38 organizations in the study, the best achieved A-level internal hires 18% of the time, and the worst only 1% of the time.[3] Especially for critical roles, it is essential to track quality of both internal and external hires.

Both outcomes can be tracked in the same way with comparable data using the WQI. The result is an index that expresses quality weighted for productivity in all roles being measured. The index is broken down to the lowest component level (the individual) and sliced to provide any view desired for which corresponding data exist. For example:

- Source of highest quality hires sorted by industry

- Quality of hire sorted by business unit

- Quality of internal versus external hires

- Quality of internal hires completing leadership program

- Quality of hire (total is current versus prior period)

The WQI itself should be calculated periodically (yearly, for example) using talent movement (hires and internal placements) after 24 months in a role. Because a numerical value is assigned to both performance and potential ratings and advancement and retention are "yes or no" factors, the ability to automate the computation of Hires/Placements by Quality Level from files storing these data is simplified.

As Fig. 4.5 shows, once a base year is established, future years can be compared to determine improvement or decline in the WQI. In this way, the WQI becomes the focal point for adjusting talent plans with the goal of increasing the index value.

The data underlying the WQI provide the ability to analyze talent activity from a number of vantage points. By doing so, organizations can evaluate which talent acquisition, development, or retention changes will be most likely to have a positive impact on the index. Fig. 4.6 depicts how that analysis might impact the talent plan.

---

[3] Identifying drivers of internal transfer performance, a quantitative analysis. Corporate Executive Board, 2004.

Quality Level	2017 Movement @ 24 months			2018 Movement @ 24 months			2019 Movement @ 24 months		
	Hires	Productivity Factor	Weighted Hires	Hires	Productivity Factor	Weighted Hires	Hires	Productivity Factor	Weighted Hires
SUPER STAR (12X)	2	12	24	7	12	84	9	12	108
STAR (3X)	22	3	66	38	3	114	42	3	126
AVERAGE (1X)	90	1	90	69	1	69	68	1	68
BELOW (−1X)*	6	−1	−6	4	−1	−4	4	−1	−4
Total	120		174	118		263	123		298
Quality Index		1.450			2.229			2.423	
Quality Index %Δ					54%			9%	

* Includes anyone who has exited the organization

Fig. 4.5.   Calculate the Weighted Quality Index (WQI).

Talent quality has a direct impact on the creation and value of intellectual capital, usually more than 50% – and sometimes higher than 90% – of the value of any corporation. Talent quality increases successful outcomes of business investments more than any other factor. Monitoring and adjusting talent investments in order to improve the WQI leads to positive returns on investment.

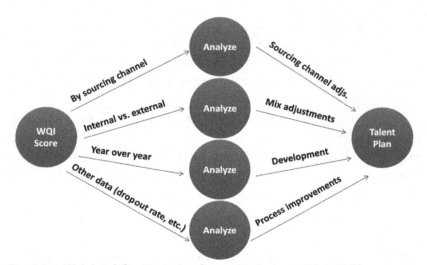

Fig. 4.6.   Weighted Quality Index Score Analysis and Talent Plan.

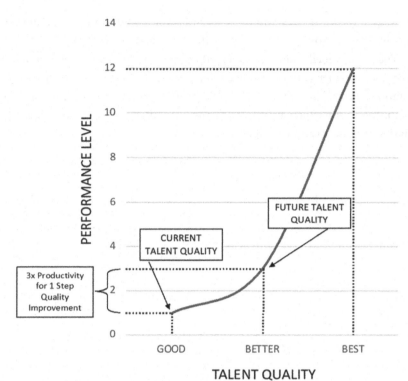

Fig. 4.7. Exponential Performance Curve.

Is measuring quality in this way worth the time and effort?

Considering the exponential jump in productivity as quality notches up – quite extreme in complex professional jobs – the value difference is surely worth the time and effort. Just considering the value of what you are paying the talent, let alone the commercial value of their output, the numbers should be convincing. As depicted in Fig. 4.7, for a jump from an average performer to a star performer the research suggests a 3x improvement in productivity (for a super-star it is 12x). Let's say you are paying a team of engineers $5 million in annual compensation. For a relatively small gain in quality from good (average) to better (star), you get the equivalent of what it would cost to simply triple the size of the team, i.e., $10 million in value. Who can afford to leave that value on the table? Done well, a sound talent strategy for critical roles will more often be able to hit home runs and even get the 12x improvements. This can all be tracked via the WQI.

The value added from a commercial output standpoint will be even more extreme. Whether you are producing patents in the biotech industry or new solutions in the information technology field, increasing the productivity factor for a team exponentially is a financial windfall. This is what accelerates market values, it cannot be ignored!

5

CHANGING THE FILTER

Refreshing the HR Operating Model Over Time

Even the ideal HR operating model today will not withstand the test of time for very long – the lens through which the model is viewed must be attuned with the business' evolving vision of itself. Businesses are future focused, and over time the Value-Driven Talent Strategy has to evolve to keep up with this "future" as well. Changing the filter via the evolving talent strategy means updating the HR operating model to ensure execution can be sustained. In this section of the guide, we will give some examples of the types of changes that might be encountered and how to actively evolve and adjust to your own company's circumstances.

A multitude of internal and external factors impact the evolution of the HR operating model over time, for example:

INTERNAL

- New lines of business

- Mergers and acquisitions

- Divestitures

- Geographic expansion or contraction

EXTERNAL

- Talent market dynamics

- Customer trends

- Consumer behavior and preferences

- Regulatory environment

Often, particular factors affect one industry more than another and risks can be anticipated depending on what line of business your company is in – indicating what aspects of the HR operating model may require more flexibility for your circumstances.

There are a mix of considerations and options for the HR operating model that are motivated by these internal and external forces and must be periodically reexamined, including

- The critical versus supporting roles designated in the talent strategy model

- Prioritization of capability to buy, build, or borrow talent

- In-house versus outsourced HR capability and capacity

Critical versus Supporting Roles Designations

The determination of whether or not a role drives or supports value creation normally remains pretty stable over time, although significant internal or external factors can alter that; for example, a significantly different new line of business or major regulatory change could impact how drivers of business value are viewed. In rapidly evolving, knowledge-based business models such as the broad biotech industry, drivers of business value can evolve at a faster pace. For example, the criticality of scientific roles versus software development roles in these enterprises can shift fairly quickly, depending on what the nature of the final product might be or become.

Following are a few scenarios involving business decisions that might change the filter for how you think about the appropriate HR operating model:

Scenario 1

Let us imagine a biotech business that has historically been focused on the biological side of genomic sequencing and has grown its successful capability through acquiring mostly experienced and senior-level researchers, producing patented approaches to scientific applications that are important to its institutional customers. Recently, the company has identified the next big area of opportunity which would take it in the direction of specialized data technology and software development to power the exploitation of its biological knowledge and insights. Upon delving into this strategy with senior executives, it becomes very apparent to the CHRO that the talent strategy for acquiring this information technology capability in the coming years will require hiring in entry-level IT graduates and developing them internally.

This is a major shift in organizational strategy that requires a "filter change" on the HR side. The impact of the strategy would ultimately shift the shape of the company organization structure from a diamond to a pyramid (Fig. 5.1).

The kind of implications this will have for HR and the company include, for example:

• A new capability to attract and acquire new graduates and assimilate them into the company

• The need to develop retention strategies for entry-level professionals (highly sought after) in which the company will be making significant investment

• Creation of a new, prospective organization structure and hierarchy

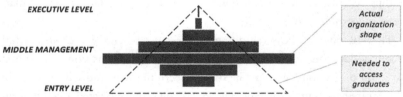

Fig. 5.1. Modifying the Organization Strategy to Access a Graduate Talent Pool.

- Design of learning and development strategies that had not previously existed

- Assimilation of a large group of younger employees into the workforce and evolution of an effective company culture

These changes and investments in new HR capabilities are required to successfully support the strategic direction of the company. This is an HR filter change; new capabilities, likely some obsolescence as well, and the agility to shift in synch with the business is imperative – simply iterating with existing HR capability as the initiative unfolds would be too high a risk.

Scenario 2

A large clinical research organization (CRO) that provides drug development services to the pharmaceutical industry employs thousands of clinical research associates (CRAs) around the world. The company's pharma customers also employ CRA talent within their own organizations to work on internal projects. The CRO has identified a new opportunity and has created a new company strategy to supply customers with CRA talent. The size of the business is deemed to be in the tens of thousands of hires annually. The CRO is continuously in the market for this talent and has reasoned that it can be lucrative financially, as well as profitable from a customer relationship standpoint to provide this service. However, due to the project nature of pharma customers' demand for CRAs, the actual hiring curve is somewhat unpredictable and will likely generate large swings from month to month. Hiring demand for the CRO has previously been very predictable and non-seasonal. Staffing its own recruiting function to meet such a fluctuating new demand curve is a problem to be solved.

The HR filter on how recruiting works must be changed to successfully accommodate this new business strategy. The CHRO has done an estimate based on projections of what the overall recruiting demand will be once the new strategy is put into play. Fig. 5.2 shows the expected overall hiring demand for the company.

Analyzing recruiting capacity on an annual basis has provided an indication of how many recruiters will be required to fulfill the new demand. But due to

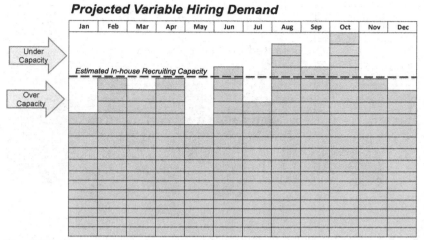

Fig. 5.2.   Projected Variable Hiring Plan.

the fluctuations expected in the new CRA business, in most months, the average recruiting capacity needed will either be too much or not enough – significantly. Both of those scenarios result in additional cost (incurred or wasted).

The solution to this new strategy – the filter change – is to employ a recruitment process outsourcing (RPO) firm to support the company's incremental recruitment work and create a flexible hiring organization. In order to attract an RPO at a reasonable rate, some of the existing recruitment volume, as well as logistics support for all hiring, will also be assigned to them. By flipping the demand curve, the CRO is able to provide a plan that produces steady, predictable capacity for the in-house recruitment team while requiring the RPO to provide the needed flexibility and avoid additional cost (Fig. 5.3).

As with Scenario 1, it is also a major shift in organizational strategy that requires a "filter change" on the HR side. The impact of the strategy would shift the size and makeup of the recruiting organization. It would also have many additional change implications, for example:

- HR capacity and capability to assess, select, and oversee the addition of a third-party service provider to the organization.

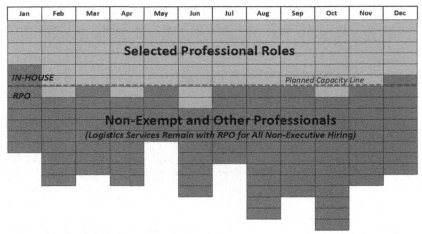

Jan	Feb	Mar	Apr	May	Jun	Jul	Aug	Sep	Oct	Nov	Dec

Selected Professional Roles

IN-HOUSE   *Planned Capacity Line*

RPO

Non-Exempt and Other Professionals
(Logistics Services Remain with RPO for All Non-Executive Hiring)

Fig. 5.3. Flexible Hiring Organization.

- HR capability to re-engineer processes to ensure the in-house and RPO recruitment efforts are integrated with and seamless for the business organization.

- Aligning technologies and users so that data and information, as well as its security, are both efficient and effective.

Word of Caution on Using Recruitment Outsourcing Firms

RPOs have a rather notorious reputation for overpromising and under-delivering, but does it have to be that way? We don't believe so.

Under the right circumstances, RPOs should be a valid alternative for supplying talent for all but the most critical roles. The caveat here of course is "the right circumstances." What are they? After years of implementing, managing, and observing these arrangements across various industries, we boil it down to three essential factors:

1. *Documented, socialized, and streamlined process management*: Of all the HR functions, recruiting is the one that lends itself most to (we would say requires) buttoned-up, transparent process. While process is sometimes

overlooked or sidestepped inside organizations that do their own recruiting, this cannot be the case with an RPO. Because it's an outsourced solution, an RPO is a step away from the main organization and process is critical to bridging that space. Detailed, yet practical, process is the glue that binds RPO, HR, and hiring managers in an effective partnership that can deliver as promised.

2. *Management of both process and results metrics*: Managing by metrics is the most powerful tool in the RPO kit. Process metrics and results metrics both serve important, yet different, purposes. Process (or interim) metrics are the key to predicting and fulfilling desired outcomes. How many candidates sourced per requisition, how many days between interview and offer, and how many requisitions per recruiter? Results metrics such as time to fill and hiring manager satisfaction inform whether or not something needs to be tweaked further downstream in the process and are usually the cornerstone of service level agreements. The targets for these metrics must be carefully thought through as they inevitably impact both the cost and the effectiveness of the RPO.

3. *Employment branding and recruitment marketing*: Employment branding is increasingly important to all businesses to cut through competitive clutter and attract the right talent. In the case of an RPO, the discipline of employment branding and how it is activated throughout the hiring process is of even higher importance. As an outsourced solution, RPOs are inevitably challenged to represent the client organization as effectively as an in-house recruiter is able to do. A well-defined and activated employment brand will solve this handicap.

An additional word of caution is that the RPO providers, with the best intentions, often offer to supply and activate all three of these levers themselves. This is the proverbial banana peel that can trip you up for two reasons. First, RPO providers have a core capability of sourcing talent, not engineering (process and metrics) or marketing (branding). Second, these are client levers that need to be created and managed in a way that ensures their full integrity, in everyone's best interest.

Having these three client levers in place, RPO can be a valid solution for many hiring situations and can provide the flexibility and expertise companies seek, while avoiding the underdelivery that too often occurs.[1]

These types of strategic talent challenges are examples that reflect how changing internal and external business conditions can require companies to evolve their own visions of themselves. In order for HR to work effectively with the CEO and his/her executive team to break through these challenges, flexibility, business acumen, and integration must prevail.

Historically HR has not been known for demonstrating these qualities. For example, in many organizations, a wall of separation has existed between the talent acquisition (TA) and talent management (TM) functions. TA often operates on its own, separate from other HR units, including TM, while bemoaning the fact that no one "gets" what they do. At the same time, HR Business Partners and TM professionals often wonder, "What do those recruiters do? How hard can recruiting be?" Even if they report into the same senior HR leader, it's not typical for these groups to work together in an integrated way or even with the same goals in mind.

The importance of integrating TA and TM is evident as the need for – and scarcity of – specialized talent becomes more critical. Influential CHROs must be dedicated to kicking these walls down once and for all and empowered to do so by the CEO. They know the old-school approach to keeping specialty teams siloed and workstreams separate just does not make sense. In some organizations, it's already coming apart at the seams as hiring managers demand faster, higher quality TA and employees demand to know what options exist for them to learn and grow in their career.

Complex talent challenges, such as the examples above, cannot be addressed if HR continues to work in functional silos, detached from overarching strategies and quantitative measurements.

What will it take to keep the HR operating model in good working order? This is the subject of the next section in this guide, Care and Maintenance.

---

[1] Talent Growth Advisors. (2017). Recruiting Process Outsourcing (RPO) can improve hiring results: Four ways to do it. Retrieved from https://talentgrowthadvisors.com/resources/blog/recruiting-process-outsourcing

6

CARE AND MAINTENANCE

Actions Taken Periodically to Keep the HR Operating Model in Good Working Order

As we've seen in "Changing the Filter," sometimes business shifts require a fundamental change to the HR operating model – essentially pivoting to a different model. It is more typical, however, that the HR operating model just requires routine care and maintenance.

With time, flaws creep into any operating model, regardless of what the model is. These can range from a buildup of costly inefficiency and waste to obsolescence that inhibits effective execution. Rather than going through a painful cycle of off-and-on HR investment which eventually leads to wholesale teardown and rebuilding, this section of the guide examines how to audit the investment on an ongoing basis, so the operating model continually supports value creation in the way it was intended to do.

This implies at least an annual introspective exercise. What part of the existing investment is foundational and what is discretionary? What can be put on hold or structured as a variable cost tied to the business cycle? Care and maintenance of the HR operating model boils down to minimizing waste and maximizing relevance. Tethering the HR operating model to sound budgeting and planning routines imbedded in the business is the key to achieving both.

Many internal and external business factors routinely affect the cost of HR investment and the relevance of spending that is taking place, including:

- Mergers, acquisitions, divestitures

- Routine business expansion or contraction

- Talent market dynamics

- Technology advancements

- Regulatory and cultural environment

Any of these factors can change what is required for the HR operating model to remain in good working order, that is:

- Having the right HR capabilities in the right places

- Having enough capacity to do the work

- Functioning as one integrated organism

- Having the agility to react quickly to immediate business needs

- Being cost competitive

MIX OF PEOPLE, PROCESS, AND TECHNOLOGY IN THE HR FUNCTION

When you think about care and maintenance of the HR operating model and the factors that cause it to require such attention, it becomes apparent that there are really only three big buckets to deal with: People, Process, and Technology.

People

While all three of these elements are essential to the capability of HR, people are the most expensive element in the mix. They also present the most opportunities for improving efficiency as technology improves and reduces the amount of manual effort to complete work. Trade-offs between efficiency and effectiveness in this mix are very important to pay attention to, especially as it impacts the support of critical roles in the company.

As noted in the last section, Changing the Filter, HR organizations are often very fragmented internally (or become so), and a serious look at constantly optimizing the mix of people, process, and technology must be viewed through this lens; waste is usually a systemic rather than localized issue within HR.

While the need for closer integration of HR activities has become evident, other stars are aligning to drive a solution. Take technology advances for example – along with the economic pressure for resource efficiency. Social networks like LinkedIn have lifted the veil on the range of available talent on a near-global scale, much like the Internet did for retail goods more than a decade ago. Prior to this visibility, organizations often used a two-phased process by which the Talent Management team scanned the organization for internal talent to fill higher-level roles, and if it were scarce, Talent Acquisition would begin the lengthier search externally. Now, with skilled TA professionals, it's possible to respond to needs more quickly with a slate of the best internal *and* external candidates.

It is worthwhile delving more deeply into the trend and need for integration between the work of talent acquisition and talent management as a primary example of rethinking the people side of the HR capability mix and performing smart maintenance on the model. As companies continue to look for ways to expand leaders' spans of control in their quest to reduce expenses, it's also a logical choice to actually combine TA and TM functions under one chief. Not only is this efficient from a cost standpoint but the synergies between the work of the two functions are an indirect benefit of this action and are no less significant.

When a group of senior HR leaders recently gathered to discuss their shared challenges in redefining the future of talent with us, an immediate focus of conversation became the integration of TA and TM. For these leaders and for leaders all across the globe, it's a conversation that is marked by urgency. For many, the opportunities for collaboration and synergy are just too great to miss, while for many others the costs of the disconnects are becoming too painful to ignore. The conversation, then, isn't *whether* to integrate the functions but *how*. And the devil, as they say, is in the details.

Most leaders acknowledge the difficulty of bringing together the two functions. It's not enough to establish a few new processes. Instead, it's about creating new roles, new behaviors, new mental models, and even new cultures. As organizational transformations go, this is difficult territory.

Based on this discussion and our own observations, it is clear that most HR leaders agree the most vexing problems associated with such an integration of Talent Management and Talent Acquisition focus on difficulty in:

- Aligning TM and TA goals in a way that aligns them with one another, and which directly supports the overall talent strategy

- Developing shared, integrated systems, metrics and processes that support TM and TA goals

- Revamping a talent organization structure that is more likely to deliver on desired results

- Defining roles and responsibilities for evolving talent jobs – and identifying/selecting for those roles

- Clarifying what "good" looks like – behaviors, skills, and outcomes – for each role

- Expanding or updating systems to manage and track accurate data along the entire talent continuum – from acquisition to retention

Secondary issues of note relate to conflict between HR generalist and TA teams, managers working outside established HR processes, overly complex or frequently changing talent processes and tools, and the revolving door of HR leaders, each of whom brings new and different priorities and approaches.

Fixing the Foundation with Competencies

Considering all these challenges – along with the complexity of driving change in any size organization – can be daunting. But best-in-class approaches begin with the end in mind by focusing on competencies: specifically, those skills and experiences necessary to get everyone on the HR team – including TM, TA, and HR partners – from here to there.

The group of senior HR leaders echoed what we've seen working with and benchmarking a variety of Fortune 1000 companies; there is widespread agreement on what skills are needed to drive success in any HR role:

- Drive for results

- Ability to make data-driven decisions

- Personal credibility

- Business acumen

- Leading through change

- Ability to select and develop talent

- HR functional knowledge (sourcing, interviewing, talent planning, etc.)

If one group of HR professionals within the overall team lacks in these skills, they lose credibility not only with business leaders within the organization but also among their HR peers. Others begin working around them and excluding them from meetings and decisions. Therefore, the importance of building skills and credibility among all of HR is seen as a critical success factor when integrating TM and TA.

The Talent Advisor: What Will It Take to Get There?

Once competencies are defined, roles and goals with HR can be more easily identified and structured. One role that has been the subject of many recent research papers, and has generated a lot of buzz, is the "Talent Advisor."

In many ways, the role seems to be one attempt to link TA and TM accountabilities. Traditional recruiters are tactical, reactive, and typically overloaded with more job requisitions than they can effectively handle. They don't usually have the time – or the skills for – influencing, negotiating, identifying longer-term talent needs, or advising hiring managers. TM professionals, on the other hand, are typically adept at talent planning, helping managers assess and manage their people, and identifying methods for engaging and retaining key talent. But they don't often get involved in making individual selection decisions. Although the two functions have the same overall goals – ensuring the organization has the best talent – the two roles just don't intersect in most organizations.

Enter the Talent Advisor. This role is a talent planning strategist, hiring manager influencer, and sourcer extraordinaire. The Talent Advisor finds, sells, and closes highly qualified, passive candidates. They counsel hiring managers regarding the best talent decisions for his/her organization. They push back on decisions that don't meet the longer-term talent needs of the business. They scan employee data to identify "ready now" as well as next-gen leaders.

Sounds great. But is it reality? Is it possible to find one (many?) who can manage the spectrum ranging from recruiting for dozens of positions to strategic talent advisor? Can one person do all that?

Possibly. In fact, a few of the HR leaders voiced success with early trials of a Talent Advisor–type position. In such organizations, they act as high-powered recruiters and also sit in on talent review meetings. They strive to manage internal pipeline and influence decision-making. Their background? Some prefer HR generalists or TM professionals who understand talent acquisition, others are using high-performing recruiters to fill the role. At any rate, the need for development is clear, lest the Talent Advisor role suffer the same early fate as HR Business Partners: when that role first came into vogue, many organizations simply changed incumbents' titles and expected their approach to the role to change simultaneously, too – it usually didn't.

The talent advisor role, then, clearly requires capabilities beyond eye-balling resumes and scheduling interviews. Skill sets aside, there are other challenges in bringing this role to life:

- Identifying the right blend of tactical and strategic talent acquisition skills for the role

- Paying salaries commensurate with such a unique and valuable skill set

- Convincing more seasoned HR professionals that this role – which typically has no direct reports – is an important career move nonetheless

- Clarifying the roles and responsibilities of the Talent Advisor vs HR Business Partners and TM professionals; where does one end and the other begin?

- Managing the complexity associated with a (typically) large number of requisitions and a variety of hiring managers

- The early indication that Talent Advisors are most successful supported by a team of researchers and/or sourcers, which may lead to a different organizational structure and increased resource requirements.

- Hiring managers who don't trust the recruiting process and who are hesitant to relinquish decision-making throughout the TA cycle (culling candidates, prescreening, selecting qualified internals, etc.)[1]

---

[1] Talent Growth Advisors. (2011). The intersection of talent acquisition and talent management. Retrieved from https://talentgrowthadvisors.com/resources /talent-acquisition-talent-management.

The preceding discussion about the evolution of a Talent Advisor role is a good example of keeping the HR operating model in good working order from a "People" standpoint. It's one of the opportunities to make the model more effective and more efficient. The thinking across the HR organization should be similar. What is the work? What is the cost? What should be more closely integrated? How can that be done better with both effect and cost?

While the people component is the costliest in the operating model, the process component is the equivalent of a musical score. The highly skilled musicians in a symphony orchestra won't amount to much without the score (and presumably a conductor). The processes – what the work is and how it will be done – provide the instructions for which HR roles will be needed, how many positions of each, what organization structure is appropriate, what tools and technology are needed, and how things will be measured.

Process

HR work, like the work of most support functions, is very process driven. Even the most mundane parts of the model, such as **Managing Benefits**, can and should be boiled down to a set of repeatable processes, including for example:

- Performing benefits market analysis

- Designing and delivering benefit plans and programs

- Administering benefits

- Performing benefits program compliance, governance, and reporting

- Performing benefits financial analysis and reporting

All of these subprocesses must be executed to manage benefits plans. For each of these subprocesses, there are a set of activities, each requiring input of some defined information and producing some output of information or final product. Information systems have blurred the lines between systems and processes, but these need to be understood separately. Process documents a strategy for doing work. Systems serve to enable the strategy and optimize its execution.

We recently had the opportunity to observe a great example of pure HR process – recruiting in the absence of any technology – at a baseball stadium on the US west coast.

An Unexpected Example of the Best Recruiting We've Seen

Our consulting team members have personally led global recruiting teams and also consulted with recruiting leaders in industries ranging from fast food to missile systems, but the most impressive recruiting execution we've yet to have seen anywhere was the stadium recruiting for a west coast baseball team.

"How mundane can you get?" you might think. Finding hundreds of warm bodies to climb unforgiving cement stairs on game day, slogging concessions, and helping disoriented fans get their tickets right side up – all for less than 10 bucks an hour.

In some stadiums we've seen, it feels like the recruiting effort involves putting an ad on Craigslist, hanging posters at bus stops, and slapping a shirt on the first few hundred folks who showed up before the game started. Not at this one.

After years of continually improving, this west coast team, under the leadership of a very bright Director – Human Resources, has nailed both customer service and employee engagement by executing a recruiting process that hits on every cylinder:

- Effective employment value proposition

- Tight candidate screening

- Excellent candidate interview and selection process

- Disciplined preemployment attention and execution

- Exceptional hiring manager involvement

- Unheard of retention statistics

All of this with (whoops!) virtually no technology.

In a business segment that normally experiences 60–80% turnover, they experience 10%. They select candidates rather than candidates selecting them. They get 100% attendance rather than 20–30% weekly no-shows.

They hire once per year instead of replenishing weekly during the season, as most other stadiums do. How did they do this?

It's people, process, and technology. In that order.

1. They have the right people on the recruiting team:

   • Motivated recruiters

   • Hiring managers and their managers

   • Current employees

2. They have a process designed for winning:

   • Attract highly motivated candidates

   • Meticulously screen in advance of interviewing

   • Efficient interviewing with the recruiting team – on time, no delays

   • Rejected interviewees treated like royalty

   • Successful interviewees hired on the spot and go home with uniforms and training schedule in hand

3. They involve new stadium hires in the brand and game day experience delivery from day one:

   • Current employees describe their role in the game day experience as part of the interview process

   • Interview day takes place in the executive level stadium suites – followed by an up close and personal stadium tour

   • Hires are provided with public transportation passes that identify them as part of the team

How about the nonexistent technology? Would it help? Sure, the right technology could grease the skids on this nearly manual, high-volume hiring operation. It might even make some worthwhile things possible that just cannot be done manually. But, the process is what works well now. Who knows? Technology might even just screw it up.

Realistically, technology is an integral part of every modern HR operating model – it is what makes a good thing a lot better...and to enable approaches to problem-solving that just were not possible in a manual world, so technology for HR is truly indispensable.

Technology

It is a no-brainer that technology on the purely transactional side of HR (payroll, benefits, employee administration, etc.) is both essential and optimal – it can deliver as advertised. Technologies to support Talent Management and Talent Acquisition, as we said, are indispensable to a degree but also often do not fully deliver as advertised. Clearly, cause for shortcomings fall on both the sellers' and the users' depending on the particular circumstances. However, too often we have observed that HR teams recoil from serious process design, while latching on to the latest and greatest technology offering – proven or unproven. Wishful thinking is not a good approach to tech investments.

Three common realities of HR technology investments are as follows:

Effectively Adding Technology Usually Takes Longer Than Anyone Expects

Making the decision to acquire technology is just one step in a very long process. Consider what's involved: influencing key stakeholders, budgeting, a request for proposal process, vendor selection, contracting, configuration, testing, implementation, training, etc. – the timeframe is often measured in years vs months. Leaders often don't even stay in their role long enough to show evidence that the technology is, in fact, adding value to the process.

Technology without Process Design May Not Even Provide an Incremental Lift

If your technology isn't configured to support a specific and detailed desired state process (which in turn supports a broader HR strategy), it simply can't work. The most advanced, perfect technology – laid on top of an unclear process in which roles and responsibilities aren't defined or desired outcomes are unclear – will never add value. Plus, once implementation begins, HR leaders often find that their chosen technology may not integrate well with other systems, or there aren't enough workflows or configuration options available, or users begin to push back because it's "too difficult" to use and the upside is unclear.

It's Too Good to Be True

As much as we want to believe it – it's just not going to work as promised during even the most compelling demo. Companies – especially those powered by intellectual capital and dependent on quality hires – simply can't avoid the hard work involved with attracting, selecting, and retaining talent – no matter how many technologies it cobbles together. The war for scarce talent is getting harder and the solution is not as quick and easy as we wish it were.

Of course, there are great HR technologies out there – and there is a time and place for them.[2]

Our observation is that technology solutions for HR are more often than not, more expensive than planned once they are installed because costs were minimized on the up-front planning and configuration effort. The impetus to buy and install these systems is often itself more a promise of lowering costs than improving talent results. Because that is the case, systems are often not well enough planned and often launched too quickly, before giving adequate strategic thought to requirements, desired outcomes and the all-important configuration.

Technology rules to live by for HR are as follows:

- Make sure fully qualified project management is in place, not just the best available

- Do not assume your organization already has sufficient subject matter expertise; this may need to be acquired

- Configure technology only from detailed process design plans that have been road tested

- Allow the time that is necessary to accurately implement the solution – underpromise and overdeliver

---

[2] Talent Growth Advisors. (2018). Talent acquisition technology isn't going to fix your hiring problems. Retrieved from https://talentgrowthadvisors.com/resources/blog/talent-acquisition-technology.

Technology investments are normally millions of dollars, if not immediately, then over a few years. This is one area where you must resist the urge to be penny wise on the up-front preparation.

NATURE OF COSTS (VARIABLE, FIXED, STEP) AND COST DRIVERS

Part of the regular care and maintenance of the HR operating model is a sound approach to building and frequently examining its financial underpinnings utilizing tools that include the following:

- Zero-based planning and budgeting

- Indexing variable costs

- Operating metrics deep analysis (evaluating waste)

Going back to a point made earlier, many HR professionals profess a love of people over a love of business. This notion is underscored by HR leaders who do not know the true cost of critical HR responsibilities such as hiring, training, turnover. In most cases, this doesn't upset them because they believe it's either not possible to get such data or such HR activities are just a "cost of doing business." Rarely do HR leaders complain about not having access to data that would allow them to evaluate and improve the cost-effectiveness of their efforts. This in and of itself is a significant problem.

In popular HR industry blogs and publications there are no shortage of articles on "ROI of HR investments" and related nonsense – nonsense because if HR typically doesn't even have knowledge of their true and complete costs, why bother?

At the same time, we also observe that most finance departments are not motivated to assist HR in creating a clear picture of their costs. This may simply be because they consider HR funding a sunk cost, a financial burden to some extent, that requires more control than management – and so far history has proven them to be right. This further reinforces HR as second-class citizens who certainly haven't earned their "seat at the table."

Here is how HR can turn the tables and provide care and maintenance to their organization at the same time.

Zero-Based Planning and Budgeting

This is the opposite of asking for incremental (or being directed to decremental) funding. On the inside of HR, it regularly resets the required cost of supporting the company business plan, adjusted for any efficiencies to be realized or value-added investments made. It pinpoints obsolescence and redundancy that can be addressed within the HR organization. Outside of HR, it ultimately creates credibility and honest brokering with the rest of the company.

Zero based means "starting" with zero resources each planning period (e.g., each year) and building up the proposed HR plan and budget based on planned activity, from scratch. The HR operating model, assuming no filter change, remains pretty stable in terms of the work that is done. It then becomes a matter of anticipating throughput for the model based on the business' own plans and need for support. There is an intersection here with Workforce Planning discussed in Chapter 2 of this guide.

If you think of costs being categorized as people, process, and technology, it is fairly straightforward to build up a zero-based plan from there.

Let's use talent acquisition as an example.

We stated earlier in this section that process is the equivalent of a musical score to an orchestra – this is the right starting point to define the work and build up an accurate view of resources that are required to complete it, given a set of objective assumptions.

The big process buckets for recruiting are typically these:

- Planning

- Recruitment

- Selection

- Offer and Acceptance

- Onboard

The major assumptions that need to be articulated are as follows:

- Number and timing of hires (by categories to include job and job type, location, etc.)

- Expected mix of internal and external hires

- Expected mix of active and passive candidates by job

- Technology and technology changes

- Tools and tool changes (assessments, background checks, etc.)

- Outsourced services

- Productivity of in-house recruiting resources

With the process and assumptions as a backdrop, the number and type of recruiting resources can then be built up from a zero base to what is being proposed for the current planning period, providing basic analysis that describes the drivers of any increase or decrease vs prior periods. The zero-based method provides total transparency and all information that is required to assess the risks and likelihood that the plan will hold up in reality.

Indexing Variable Costs

A substantial portion of HR cost is variable, that is, it will trend higher or lower with volume changes. An easy example of this is recruiting work. Although technologies have helped improve the productivity of recruiters, if hiring volume goes up significantly, it will require more recruiters – and more money to post jobs to external job boards – to do the work at the same level of performance. Other roles in HR are not very sensitive to volume changes – the Benefits Plans Administrator will not require additional capacity even if the organization served doubles in size (at some point if the number of benefits plans expand, that may require more capacity).

It is important to index certain positions to levels of output when they are sensitive to those movements so that costs can be accurately planned for, higher or lower, depending on changes in activity. These are also the roles for which some portion of capacity may be outsourced to contract workers, especially if wide swings in activity are anticipated or often occur in the normal course of business.

In the absence of recognizing which costs are variable and which are fixed, HR departments establish financial guidelines that end up being unnecessarily disruptive to the HR operating model.

Operating Metrics Deep Analysis

Inevitably, waste and obsolescence build up in any operating model with the passage of time. Sometimes this is obvious, and the situation can be dealt with before too much cost is incurred. Often, these costs go unnoticed for a longer period of time if other procedures are not activated to detect them.

We discussed the utility of operating metrics in gauging how well HR processes are working in the *Controls* section of this guide. By looking at quantitative data that indicate the efficiency and effectiveness of a process, operating metrics provide the information to solve problems that ultimately impact results metrics. By regularly doing deep analysis on operating metrics that have significantly deteriorated, HR organizations can identify waste that can be eliminated before it has cost too much.

In order to be able to flag operating metrics that should be more deeply analyzed, care must be given to assigning targets to these metrics during business planning that reflect improvements and investments that have been made. Through this practice of anticipating better performance from continuous improvement, actual data will show trends against what was expected and what has happened in the past.

Fig. 6.1 shows some examples of waste that can occur in the recruiting process, many of which can be detected through analysis, based on the "8 Wastes" framework used in manufacturing environments. This model can be defined and used for all areas in HR.

Let's examine a few ways that waste can be detected.

A typical operating metric for recruitment is time to fill jobs (TTF). This metric usually measures the amount of time between the time a job requisition is approved and the time an offer is accepted. If this time unexpectedly increases above the planned time and even above the TTF from prior periods, analysis could uncover some forms of waste that are involved with the issue. Here are some examples:

- An issue with job posting accuracy that has slowed the flow of qualified candidates (Defect)

- Offer letters are being produced differently now and often contain errors (Defect)

Type of Waste	What is it?	Generic Examples	Talent Acquisition Examples
1. Over-production	Producing too much or too soon	• Information sent automatically even when not required • Processing items before they are required by the next person in the process	• Extraneous reports distributed • Requiring candidates to complete lengthy on-line applications during the initial apply process
2. Defects	Errors, mistakes, poor quality, missed expectations	• Incorrect data entry • Incorrect name printed on a credit card • Surgical errors	• Incorrect requisition data entered • Inaccurate job postings • Incorrect offer letters sent out
3. Inventory	Holding more inventory (material and information) than required	• Excess promotional material sent to the market • Overstocked medicines in a hospital • More servers than required	• Uncoordinated sourcing efforts • Simultaneous internal/external candidate search • Designed but unused talent programs (referral, etc.)
4. Over-Processing	Processing more than required – misunderstanding customer requirements	• Too much paperwork for a mortgage loan • Same data required in number of places in a form • Follow-ups and costs associated with coordination • Too many approvals	• Numerous approvals required for requisitions • Excessive number of interviews or interviewers • Additional approvals required prior to offers made
5. Transportation	Movement of items more than required within or between processes	• Movement of files and documents to and from locations • Excessive e-mail attachments • Multiple hand-offs	• Assembling and mailing paper documents (rather than digital) • Printing, collating, storing of physical folders for closed requisitions
6. Waiting	Unbalanced process resulting in employees, customers, etc., waiting	• Customers waiting to be served by a contact center • Queue in a grocery store • System downtime	• Candidates waiting at different stages of process • Managers waiting • Recruiters waiting
7. Motion	Movement of people that does not add value	• Looking for data and information • Looking for surgical instruments • Movement of people to and from filing, fax and copy machines	• Bringing candidates on-site multiple times • Checking eligibility information on internal candidates • Follow-up with background vendors
8. Under-utilized People	Employees not leveraged to their own potential	• Limited authority and responsibility • Misuse of potential, resistance to change • Person assigned to wrong job	• Unclear roles, hand-offs in the hiring process • Recruiters screening for requirements that could be gathered via the ATS • Process differences driven by hiring manager preferences

Fig. 6.1. Operational Excellence in Talent Processes. (Applying the 8 Wastes of Lean Manufacturing Model to Talent Acquisition)

- Candidates are waiting excessive amounts of time at different stages in the process (Waiting)

- The number of approvals required for a requisition have been increased (Overprocessing)

These kinds of wastes are very often created unwittingly when process and procedural changes have been made or when personnel changes (including with third-party vendors) have occurred.

Underutilized People is another common kind of waste that can result after process and procedural changes have been made.

An accurate reading of Cost per Hire, and analysis to understand significant variances, may be the best way to ferret out waste as all forms of waste ultimately have a financial impact.

If there has not been a practice of tracking finances and looking for systemic waste in the HR organization, an effective way to approach the subject is depicted in Fig. 6.2. This approach focuses on 3 main levers to discover waste and effectively align HR resources:

1. Organization

   Right expertise in right jobs, minimized hierarchies, dynamic balancing of workloads wherever possible, efficient manpower utilization – easily adapts to ongoing change.

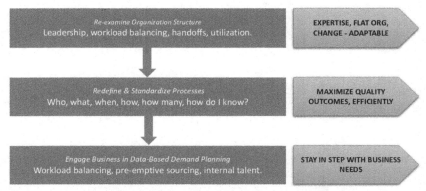

Fig. 6.2.   Steps to Address Systemic Waste in the HR Operating Model.

2. Processes

Everything built to maximize quality outcomes at the right cost –
define who does what when, how is the work done, and how is the
process communicated.

3. Demand Planning

Staying engaged and in step with the business – preemptively
ensuring the right internal and external talent; minimizing activity
that does not align with this.

CONCLUSION

Decades of research, opinions, and activities in the name of "HR Transformation" has generated, at best, iterative improvement. It is time for HR to
not only operate inside the context of the business and the way in which value
is created, but it should drive the process of doing so. This is a bridge too far
for many existing HR professionals which is why we believe the time is right
for a new function – a new capability – blending finance and HR. This book
was written as a roadmap and owner's manual for making that happen.

7

BEFORE YOU CALL

A Checklist of What to Look at before Calling the Consultants

Let's face it, more often than not, calling the consultants results in being advised to take actions that you already knew were necessary (but for some reason did not take). This chapter provides CEOs and CHROs with a checklist of symptoms they may observe when something is awry across the HR operating model. For each symptom, we offer common causes and advisement regarding where to begin the process of addressing. Some of these are easily corrected, while some are more involved (Table 7.1).

In any event, beginning here can ensure the proper next steps are identified – whether that includes engaging a consulting team or not.

Problem categories with troubleshooting tips include the following:

- Hiring

- Onboarding

- Performance management

- Development

- Engagement

- Retention

- Diversity

- Costs

Table 7.1. Troubleshooting List.

Problem Experienced	Common Causes	What to Check
Hiring		
We are interviewing too many unqualified candidates	• Low availability of desired skill set in the marketplace • Qualifications are unrealistic • Not sourcing through the appropriate channels • Job ads are unclear or inaccurate • Candidates are not being properly screened	• Market survey of available talent by skill set • Talent sourcing planning process • Process for screening applicants • Recruiters' ability to source and screen candidates
New hire quality is not satisfactory	• Roles not properly defined or accurately advertised • Screening or interviewing practices are ineffective • Disconnect between how the job is positioned and the reality of the job • Onboarding practices are undefined, missing, or ineffective • Leaders' role in selection, onboarding, and/or training is unclear	• Attrition data by timeframe, role, geography • Talent attraction and screening practices • Interview and selection protocols • Onboarding and new hire training practices

Takes too long to fill open roles

- Activities and desired timeframes in the recruiting process, including hand-offs, are unclear
- Time-consuming steps exist such as excessive approvals, manual work, requirements to keep job requisitions open, etc.
- Pipelining and aggressive sourcing activities are not proactively in place for low availability roles
- Managers can change the specs of the role, request more candidates, etc., without understanding the talent marketplace and consequences
- Ancillary processes like job requisition approval, offer creation, background checking, equity analysis, etc., add significant delays

- "Total Vacancy Time" rather than only "Time to Fill" in order to measure and analyze the total elapsed time between a role becoming vacant through the time a new hire starts
- Number of systems, integrations, tools, approvals, and hand-offs involved in the end-to-end hiring process
- Ease and simplicity of approvals and hand-offs throughout the process
- Timeframes within which managers respond to their tasks throughout the process (including in-take meetings, resume reviews, interviews, offer extensions, etc.)

Not enough candidates apply

- Recruitment marketing activities are ineffective
- Job descriptions are unrealistic
- Job ads are benign, not compelling
- Passive candidate sourcing techniques are missing or ineffective
- Recruitment marketing efforts do not account for or address marketplace concerns about the job or the company

- Analysis of the availability of talent in the marketplace for the skills required
- Whether the jobs are defined and advertised appropriately/effectively
- Sourcing plans for the skills needed that encompass active and passive candidate sources
- Programs such as referral and rehire executed in a targeted way
- Awareness throughout the organization about the needs

Table 7.1. (Continued)

Problem Experienced	Common Causes	What to Check
Too many candidates apply	• Job descriptions/ads describe requirements that are too low • Recruitment marketing efforts are too expansive • Company is perceived to be a great employer or jobs are perceived to be highly desirable • Automated candidate screening tools are not in place • Referral program is not effectively targeted	• State of minimum requirements for positions as defined in the job description and job ad • Existence of adequate screening questions within the applicant tracking system • Reassess recruiting avenues by which candidates are applying – e.g., referral program, job boards, etc. • Build a more targeted and strategic recruitment marketing plan
Hiring managers are making poor selection decisions	• Lack of process clarity and rigor • Lack of selection tools and protocol • Lack of training • Lack of time, commitment, prioritization	• Analyze data related to number of candidates screened, interviewed, offered, dropped out/declined, turned down. Identify process improvement areas based on these data. • Improve the clarity and effectiveness of the process steps up to and including interviewing and selection • Assess the protocol and tools supporting selection decision-making • Revamp hiring manager training to enable a just-in-time, simple method for improving hiring managers skills

Onboarding

Onboarding does not happen consistently

- Process is not clearly defined, simple to administer, or documented
- Roles and responsibilities are not clear or the work falls largely on only one party (e.g., the new hire or HR, etc.)
- Key onboarding activities and results are not documented in a tracking system
- New hires are left to largely drive their onboarding process
- Process is a "one-size-fits-all" approach that is not suitable for all new hires

- Onboarding process defined based on both efficiency and effectiveness
- Onboarding documentation, including specific activities, roles, data capture, deadlines, etc.
- Use of technology to support the process including completion rates, timeframes, dashboard/reporting by leader, etc.
- Use of data to track results
- Expectations for how specific stakeholders (e.g., hiring managers, HR partners, etc.) are involved in onboarding
- Managers accountabilities for completion of onboarding aspects that are critical to new hire success rates

Onboarding activities cannot be tracked

- Onboarding process is manual, paper-based
- Technology is not used sufficiently to support the process
- Managers are primarily responsible for implementing and following up
- HR is primarily responsible for implementing and following up

- Standards and expectations regarding onboarding activities, roles, outcomes, completion dates, etc., should be clearly documented
- Technology supporting the process (or lack thereof)
- Communication to stakeholders regarding expectations and desired outcomes

Table 7.1. (Continued)

Problem Experienced	Common Causes	What to Check
New hires do not get the information, tools, and access they need	• Process may be a "one-size-fits-all" approach that is not suitable for all new hires • Manual or paper-based process may lead to things falling through the cracks • Lack of documentation clarifying who needs what and when it is needed by • Onboarding overloaded into one day or massive information dump	• Defined new hire needs (information, tools, technology, access, etc., preferably by job type, location, level, etc.) • List of information needed by new hires – e.g., must know, should know, nice to know, etc. • Current way new hires get the information they need – e.g., training, communication, signature, etc. • The way onboarding works, and the amount and type of information needed by role
Performance Management Leaders do not consistently hold teams accountable for driving results	• Gaps in performance management process direction • Lack of understanding expectations and desired outcomes • Lack of objective goals, data, and desired outcomes for individuals and teams • Lack of training	• How the process ties from individual performance to desired outcomes for both teams and the enterprise • Documentation of expected standards, process steps, roles, and outcomes • Effectiveness and accessibility of performance management training • Other available training for leaders who need to learn more about goal setting, holding teams accountable, methods for driving results

| The performance review process does not lead to value-added employment decisions such as promotions, development, etc. | • Gaps in performance management process direction
• Lack of clear methods for assessing individual performance
• Lack of accessible database to capture performance review results and decisions
• Unclear methodology for connecting performance reviews to employment decisions | • Performance review process for capturing decisions related to promotability and estimated timeframes
• Assess what currently happens with performance review results. How are results used, by whom, and when?
• How data related to performance, potential, promotability, etc., are captured and used
• Steps that are taken to integrate talent acquisition and talent management so that internal talent can be considered before roles are posted
• How senior leaders model the performance review process as a way to improve business results |
| Leaders do not provide appropriate feedback and coaching | • Lack of process clarity and rigor
• Lack of feedback methods, tools, and protocol
• Lack of leader training regarding how to set goals and give feedback
• Lack of time, commitment, prioritization | • Performance review process methods, tools, and data capture regarding feedback loops throughout the year
• Documented expectations for leader feedback delivery
• Existing methods for capture and use of data related to feedback and performance improvement
• How leaders sponsor and model feedback and coaching as a way to improve business results |

Table 7.1. (Continued)

Problem Experienced	Common Causes	What to Check
Development		
Succession plans do not exist for key roles	• Lack of connection between performance management, development planning, and employment decisions • Lack of succession planning process, stakeholder involvement, tools, training • Unclear prioritization of roles for succession planning • Inconsistent support and prioritization of succession planning	• Identification of roles for succession planning • Documentation of process, tools, plans, and outcomes for succession • Documented expectations for succession planning • Data related to succession planning efforts and discussions
Lack of robust internal pipelines of talent	• Unclear pipelining priorities/targeted roles • Clarity and rigor of internal development process • Lack of development methods, tools, and protocol • Lack of leader training with respect to developing team members • Lack of coordination between talent acquisition and talent management	• The internal talent pipelining/development process, including targets, definitions, and documentation • Pipelining goals and priorities • Pipelining data and analysis • Leader communication regarding pipelining expectations and desired outcomes • Coordination between talent acquisition and talent management teams with respect to internal talent

Unclear results from training and development investments

- Training and development efforts are disconnected from critical business outcomes
- Priorities and outcomes are undefined
- Number of training activities are measured rather than outcomes
- Training and development data are not consistently captured

- Expected training and development-related business outcomes and current priorities
- The plan for measuring effectiveness and cost of development efforts
- Method for currently capturing T&D data

Employees are not consistently meeting the requirements for their job

- Jobs may not be accurately defined
- Employees not understanding the requirements of the job or performance expectations
- Employees may not have the tools, information to do the job effectively
- Employees may lack effective training

- Documented performance standards/outcomes for jobs
- Linkage between onboarding and training to key requirements of jobs
- Employee access to necessary tools and information

Engagement

Change management efforts are not working; new initiatives not understood/ embraced fast enough

- No cohesive, structured approach to driving change initiatives
- Lack of support for investing in the time and resources required to drive change
- Poor or no understanding of the value in driving change proactively/strategically vs waiting for it to happen organically

- The existing approach and how it measures and evaluates outcomes
- Analysis of the value of investing in the resources required to drive change rapidly and successfully vs waiting for it to happen organically
- The structure, rigor, and measurements in use to execute change management
- Resources dedicated to implementing the current change management approach

Table 7.1. (Continued)

Problem Experienced	Common Causes	What to Check
Engagement results are poor	• Some leaders are ineffective • Standards for leadership, communication, and development are unclear • Accountability for retention, engagement, and performance is unknown or inconsistent • Hiring decisions are not achieving best fit with the organization	• The pattern of engagement results, where pockets of engagement are high vs low, prioritization of engagement efforts and use of best practices • The end-to-end hiring process • Market pay comparative surveys • Effectiveness of existing onboarding and training efforts • Analysis of employee engagement results and grouping of themes
Retention Turnover is too high	• Wrong people being hired (sourcing, assessment, selection) • Compensation is not competitive • Manager practices • Work environment • Ineffective onboarding • Work schedule	• Current documentation of turnover priorities • End-to-end hiring process • Market pay comparative survey • Training and development investments • Employee engagement results and patterns • Onboarding process effectiveness
Turnover is too low	• Unclear or undocumented job requirements and expectations • Performance management practices are absent or ineffective • Talent review processes are lacking or ineffective • Dysfunctional leadership practices	• Analysis of, and priorities for, low turnover areas • Details and accuracy of existing job descriptions • Effectiveness and objectiveness of the performance management and talent review processes • Leadership expectations, accountabilities, and evaluation practices

Diversity

Issue	Causes	Solutions
External candidate slates lack diversity	• Candidate sourcing is not geared to finding diverse candidates • Employment value proposition is not attracting diverse candidates	• Clarity of diversity hiring goals • Recruiter sourcing skills • Diversity plan and connection to recruiting strategy
External hires lack diversity	• Candidate pool diversity is not meeting quality standards • Hiring process is unattractive to diverse candidates	• Recruiter sourcing skills • Recruiting diversity strategy • Candidate screening procedures
Turnover rates are high among diverse employees	• Employment value proposition (EVP) regarding diversity is not being realized ("promise" is not being kept) • Management practices are not seen as being fair and transparent	• Strategy and execution for bringing the EVP to life • Diversity training and awareness among managers • Policies and communication regarding diversity expectations
Organization has significant diversity gaps in particular areas	• Unclear diversity goals • Manager motivation lacking • Low availability of diverse candidates in marketplace	• Clarity of diversity hiring goals • Recruiter sourcing skills • Recruiting diversity strategy • Diversity plan and connection to recruiting strategy • Diversity training and awareness among managers • Policies and communication regarding diversity expectations

Table 7.1. (Continued)

Problem Experienced	Common Causes	What to Check
Costs Cost of hiring is too high	• Recruiting organization structure is inefficient • Technology investments are not productive • Recruiting management lacks financial skills • Recruitment processes are not streamlined and create waste	• Recruiting budget and tracking management routines • Inventory of technology investments and their usage • State of recruiting process documentation and operating metrics • Recruitment dashboard and metrics analysis
Recruiter productivity is low	• Inefficient process design • Technology limitations • Recruiter metrics not being managed	• State of recruiting process documentation and operating metrics management • Recruiter-level metrics analysis • Alignment of recruiters to organization being supported
Search firm usage and cost is very high	• Hiring managers working outside of recruiting process • Lack of sophisticated in-house recruiter skills • Lack of planning recruitment demand	• Policy regarding search firm usage • Talent acquisition organization structure and skills • Planning routines for hard-to-find talent in the organization

Cost of human resources work is not transparent

- Spending is fragmented across HR and multiple business units
- HR leadership lacking financial management skills
- Business planning does not adequately include HR organization

- HR leadership planning and budgeting routines
- Degree of decentralized HR spending across organization
- Corporate business planning requirements for HR

ROI on HR investments is unclear

- HR goals and objectives are not clear
- HR results are not adequately measured against goals and objectives
- Talent prioritization is not clearly articulated for the company
- HR spending is not comprehensively tracked and analyzed

- HR leadership planning and budgeting routines
- Corporate business planning requirements for HR
- Existence of specific talent priorities, plans, and metrics connected to expected business value creation

Outsourced HR services cost is escalating

- Service providers are not adequately managed
- Processes for providing services are inefficient
- Volume of outsourced transactions is unexpectedly increasing

- HR organization structure for managing outsourced services
- Outsourced services management routines (quarterly reviews, etc.)
- Workforce planning and budgeting routines
- Cost per transaction metrics and analysis

GLOSSARY

Book Value Book value is a company's equity value as reported in its financial statements. The book value figure is typically viewed in relation to the company's stock value (market capitalization) and is determined by taking the total value of a company's assets and subtracting any of the liabilities the company still owes.

Business Combination Accounting A set of formal guidelines describing how assets, liabilities, noncontrolling interest, and goodwill must be reported by a purchasing company on its Consolidated Statement of Financial Position.

Contingent Workers Nonemployees contracted directly or through an agency to perform work for a temporary period of time. Distinct from outsourced services, individuals are supervised by a company manager as if they were permanent employees, although being employees of the agent or self-employed.

Enterprise Value Enterprise value (EV) is a measure of a company's total value, often used as a more comprehensive alternative to equity market capitalization. EV includes in its calculation the market capitalization of a company but also short-term and long-term debt as well as any cash on the company's balance sheet.

Free Agent Any worker who is not subject to full employment by a company; may be an individual practitioner who is working full-time or a temporary resource. All contingent workers are counted within the Free Agent description.

Human Capital The present discounted value of the additional productivity over and above the product of skilled labor, of people with skills and qualifications.[1] Human capital is owned by those people.

Intellectual Capital Means of productivity derived from certain intangible assets; a subset of intangible assets.

Intellectual Property Private property rights in ideas (for example, copyright and patents).[2]

Intangible Assets Assets of an enterprise that cannot be seen or touched. These assets include goodwill, patents, trademarks, and copyright.[3]

---

[1] Oxford Dictionary of Economics, Black J., Oxford University Press, 1997.
[2] Oxford Dictionary of Economics, Black J., Oxford University Press, 1997.
[3] Oxford Dictionary of Economics, Black J., Oxford University Press, 1997.

Knowledge Worker   Executives, professionals, and employees who know how to put knowledge to productive use; owns both the "means of production" and the "tools of production."[4]

Talent   People having the skills and abilities to fill specific professional roles.

Note:
*Terms are defined as used in the context of this book which are printed in **bold** italics throughout.*

---

[4] Post-Capitalist Society, Peter Drucker, HarperBusiness 1993.

INDEX